SAN
ANTONIO
Portrait of the Fiesta City

SUSANNA NAWROCKI *&* GERALD LAIR
PHOTOGRAPHY BY MARK LANGFORD
FOREWORD BY CLAUDE STANUSH

Voyageur Press

Special thanks for assistance with the photographs to the San Antonio Fiesta Commission, Office of Public Affairs at Kelly Air Force Base, San Antonio Conservation Society, San Antonio Charro Association, Las Casas Foundation, Rivercenter, Fiesta Texas, San Antonio Botanical Garden, and San Antonio Zoological Society.

Edited by Sara Saetre and Elizabeth Knight
Cover designed by Helene Jones
Typesetting by Peregrine Publications

Printed in Hong Kong
93 94 95 96 5 4 3 2

Library of Congress Cataloging-in-Publication Data

Nawrocki, Susanna, 1938–
San Antonio: portrait of the fiesta city / Susanna Nawrocki and Gerald Lair ; photographs by Mark Langford.
p. cm.
ISBN 0-89658-200-0
ISBN 0-89658-204-3 (pbk.)
1. San Antonio (Tex.)—History. 2. San Antonio (Tex.)—Description—Guide-books.
3. Architecture—Texas—San Antonio.
I. Lair, Gerald, 1947– . II. Langford, Mark, 1957– . III. Title.
F394.S2N39 1992   91–40861
976.4'351—dc20   CIP

Published by Voyageur Press, Inc.
P.O. Box 338, 123 North Second Street
Stillwater, MN 55082 U.S.A.
Minnesota and Canada 612-430-2210
Toll-free 800-888-9653

Voyageur Press books are also available at discounts for bulk quantities for educational, fundraising, premium, or sales-promotion use. For details contact the marketing department. Please write or call for our free catalog of publications.

Contents

Foreword

When people come to San Antonio for the first time, they are nearly always surprised. Many visitors have a vision, derived from motion pictures, of a city set in desert country, bare and sun-browned; once here, they are delighted by the lushness and greenery. Many have an image of the Alamo, also derived from the movies, as a solitary stone fort set somewhere on an open prairie; a recent visitor from San Francisco couldn't believe his eyes when he stepped out of the Hyatt Regency Hotel at nighttime and saw that famous Citadel of Liberty in front of him in the heart of downtown, its white walls luminous and magical under a focus of floodlights. Most visitors have heard of San Antonio as one of America's four unique cities; they are nearly always surprised at how different it really is, in almost every way.

When asked to write this foreword, I was surprised too. Guidebooks are useful for finding your way around cities but usually give only a sketchy view of a city's history and even less about the life and character of its citizens. What attracted me about this particular book is that while it tells tourists what to see and experience in this unusual city, it also tells San Antonians things about their city and themselves that will both surprise and enlighten them.

As a native of San Antonio who has lived in several other cities, I have heard San Antonio's alluring call. This city, known as the "soul" or "mother" of Texas, has a way of capturing visitors and enticing them to stay.

When the Spaniards came to Texas in the early eighteenth century, it was the San Antonio River (then called "Yanaguana" by the Indians living in the area) and the springs at its source (still flowing behind Incarnate Word College) that made them settle here. At the center of this first settlement was a *presidio*, or military installation (now Military Plaza with our City Hall in the center), and five Roman Catholic missions were built at intervals along the river to convert and civilize the nomadic Indians of South Texas. What is a surprise, even to many San Antonians, is that the Alamo originally was not a fort but was one of these missions.

Visitors confused by the city's winding streets often ask whether they were laid out on cow trails or by drunken citizens trying to find their way home. The answer is more logical. The first settlers were given narrow strips of land stretching back from the river from which they drew water to drink and to irrigate their

From Losoya Street in front of the Hyatt Regency Hotel, visitors can look along the Paseo del Alamo, a walkway cut between Alamo Plaza and the San Antonio River, for a dramatic view of the Alamo. In December, the city's official Christmas tree appears to dwarf the ancient mission-fort.

crops. The early roads connecting the narrow strips of land necessarily followed the meandering course of the river, and eventually became the city's streets. Today, if the streets are confusing, the river itself winding through San Antonio's downtown is one of its most charming features. Locals as well as tourists love the cobblestone walks along the river banks, the shops and restaurants, and the Parisian atmosphere.

My great-grandparents and grandparents came to San Antonio from Poland in the post–Civil War period to escape Europe's recurring wars and to find opportunities denied them in the "old country." Other immigrants—from Germany, Czechoslovakia, Ireland, Italy—came here for similar reasons. These early immigrants naturally settled in little enclaves where they could still speak their own languages and continue the customs they brought with them from their native lands.

In the various ethnic enclaves of San Antonio, people tended to keep to themselves, sometimes resenting members of other ethnic groups. HemisFair, with its slogan "The Confluence of Cultures," placed emphasis on the positive contributions of the more than thirty-two ethnic groups in San Antonio and did much to overcome negative feelings between groups. Even more so, the creation of the Institute of Texan Cultures during HemisFair provided a common meeting ground for the city's ethnic groups, engendering a mutual respect that has been enhanced by the Institute's annual Texas Folklife Festival.

San Antonio represents a confluence of cultures in another important way. It is the nexus of three very different geophysical regions. If you fly from Dallas to San Antonio, you can see distinctly the Balcones Fault, which divides East Texas with its more abundant rainfall, farms, and forests from West Texas with its scant rainfall, scrubby brush, and vast ranches. South of San Antonio there is a third geographic area, the Brush Country, fading off into the coastal plains, and then the Gulf of Mexico to the east and the country of Mexico to the southwest.

It is these three geographical areas which determine and define three distinct cultures meeting in San Antonio. The city is as far north as the Hispanic-Mexican culture advanced in the eighteenth and nineteenth centuries before it was halted by the Comanche Indians; as far west as the Southern culture came with its cotton plantations, Southern cuisine, and folkways; and as far east as the open-range Cattle Kingdom

came with its cowboy, ranch, and horse culture.

Even though Texas won its independence from Mexico in 1836, San Antonio has never given up its early Mexican culture. Today the city's population is more than 50 percent Hispanic. You can hear Spanish spoken on radio, TV, and almost any street corner, and you can see it on signs and advertisements. The Mexican national holidays Cinco de Mayo and Diez y Seis are celebrated, Mexican food is the dominant cuisine, and almost every celebration includes Mexican mariachis or conjunto music. Mexican architecture is seen everywhere, particularly in red tile roofs and Saltillo tile floors.

When the Comanches halted the Hispanic-Mexican movement north, the government in Mexico City invited American settlers into the Texas province to bolster its defenses. Many came from the Southern states through Louisiana. Their Southern culture is seen in the Greek Revival architecture, the local taste for smoked ham and hush puppies, organizations like the Texas Cavaliers, the queen and duchesses of the annual Fiesta celebrations, and remnant Rebel drawls and attitudes.

Ranch and cowboy culture imported into Texas from Mexico spread to the rest of the United States from San Antonio and the Brush Country. When I was a kid my family had a ranch near Pleasanton (about thirty-five miles south of San Antonio) that we believe was part of Mission San Jose's Rancho del Atascosa, one of the very first ranches in Texas and in the United States. In the center of Pleasanton there is a statue of a cowboy with the legend that here was born the American ranching industry. The Spaniards brought their longhorn cattle and their *vaqueros* (the forerunners of American cowboys) to this region from Mexico; later, after the Civil War, Texas cowboys not only drove Texas longhorns to railroads in Kansas to supply the Eastern states with beef but drove them to nearly all of the Western states to provide seed stock for the great American ranching industry.

On our ranch was an old bowlegged cowboy, Alex Morose, who had driven cattle up the trail when he was only fourteen or fifteen. He had slept outside so long that he could never get used to sleeping in a bed, so he slept on the wooden floor of his room. San Antonio was the headquarters city for many of those old trail-drivers, and their annual conventions were held in the Gunter Hotel. Today there is an Old Trail-Drivers Museum next to the Witte Museum in

Brackenridge Park that tells their history and exhibits their clothing and equipment, six-shooters, and rifles. But the legendary ten-gallon hat, leather or canvas jacket, and leather chaps and gauntlets of the cowboy were not designed for show; they were worn for protection against the dense, thorny chaparral of the Brush Country.

If the old-time cowboys are gone today, their culture and folkways are still strong in San Antonio. I hardly know anybody here, with or without money, who doesn't have a secret yearning to own a ranch. Young and old love to wear cowboy hats, boots, and big belt buckles. Ranching clothes come out of the closet during the annual Livestock Show & Rodeo each February. And what would a typical Texas meal be without barbecue and beans?

The juncture of the three geographical zones makes San Antonio a unique city in still another way. Its flora and fauna represent all three regions; here you find Southern pines, magnolias, and azaleas, dry-country yuccas, cacti, and palms, and tropical red-flowered hibiscus. The area is a paradise for bird-lovers, for Texas as a whole has some 540 of the nation's 700 bird species, and a large percentage of these can be seen in San Antonio at one time or another. Countless species of butterflies live here most of the year, while others pass through in migration north or south. One day, on the Guadalupe River north of San Antonio, my wife and I saw a big cypress tree aflutter with as many migrating Monarch butterflies as leaves.

Finally, what makes San Antonio so different from most other cities is its authenticity, reflected in its architecture, celebrations, and daily life. The Alamo was not put up for show. Its solid look and its nicked, weathered walls tell you that it stood for something other than nicking tourists. It is this very character that makes it Texas's most popular tourist attraction. The charm of the other downtown buildings and the River Walk has grown out of the city's history and the concern for beauty and authenticity held by the San Antonio Conservation Society and the citizens. Even the details of the buildings—the carved stone, the wrought iron, the intricate woodwork—came out of the skills and sweat of the many craftspeople who arrived first as immigrants and then settled here for good. Various vested interests greedy for tourist dollars have done their best to put a shiny veneer over the city's authenticity, but citizens have consistently fought such efforts. It is still true that what is most attractive to people about San Antonio, to citizens and tourists alike, is that most of what you see here is for real.

With industrialization, of course, San Antonio's craftspeople found fewer and fewer markets for their skills. But the various craft traditions have been continued in the Southwest Craft Center housed in the old limestone-walled Ursuline Convent where my mother went to school as a young girl. The city also has a tradition of fine art. From the time of Texas's independence on, San Antonio's natural beauty and exotic character made it especially attractive to artists of all kinds—painters, sculptors, potters, writers. Like the immigrant craftsmen, the early artists came mostly from Europe, but unlike them they came primarily from the upper classes and were trained in some of Europe's best art schools. Their documentation of San Antonio in its various stages of development now gives us a deepened sense of our history as well as an historical appreciation for art that continues in our fine art museums and in the many artists who reside here. The aesthetic sense, along with the city's diversity and reputation for friendliness and love of celebration, have created something called "the San Antonio Style" that is different from that of any other city.

But if San Antonio's past is rich, what about its future? With a large portion of its population earning their living by hand labor, how can the city prosper in an increasingly competitive, high-tech world economy? Because of its strategic location, San Antonio has been and will continue to be a military training, supply, and command installation. Because of its year-round good weather, San Antonio will always be a center for military and civilian aviation. And its proximity to Mexico makes it a natural gateway for trade with that country. San Antonio has also become a treatment and research center for many medical specialties, including the transfer of technology from the laboratory to the marketplace.

But the city's best hopes lie in the effort it is making to develop the potential of its permanent population. Despite all the emphasis on high-tech, there is increasing demand in the world economy for well-designed products that show the artistry of human hands, and some San Antonians still seem to have a natural genius for that kind of craft. A consortium of local professionals—architects, engineers, artists, educators, marketing consultants, and venture capitalists—has initiated Design San Antonio to help create quality goods and services for which there is a demand in the world economy. To prepare its citizens for the Age of Information, the city is banking on a brand new main library and a master plan for branch libraries with electronic link-ups to other libraries not only in this country but in Mexico and other parts of the world.

When I left San Antonio at the age of twenty-six to become a correspondent and writer for *Life* magazine, I wondered if I would ever return. In the intervening years I traveled all over the world and saw many fabulous cities. Eventually, though, I had that yearning to move back to the city that I knew and came to love as a boy. When I met my wife Barbara I was living in New York and as a couple we continued to live there, though we often visited my mother in San Antonio. After one such visit, we asked each other the same question: "What would you think of moving to San Antonio?"

New York was an exciting place to live; we both loved the theater and the art galleries and museums. But San Antonio was also growing and becoming more cosmopolitan, and we felt in the flux of life there as much as in New York, perhaps more so because of better opportunities for connecting more personally with people of many different occupations. When we asked each other that question, neither of us hesitated. "Let's go," we answered at the same time. We have never regretted it.

— CLAUDE STANUSH

San Antonio is the third largest city in Texas, with a metropolitan population of just over one million people. Founded nearly three hundred years ago, the Alamo City brims with a vibrant history and a sense of unending charm. The Alamo, the River Walk, El Mercado, the missions, and countless colorful celebrations make the city a favorite destination for business people and tourists.

Introduction

Welcome to San Antonio, the Alamo City. Each year, San Antonio embraces, entertains, captivates, and charms not only its own citizens, but also millions of visitors. People come from all over the world because there's much to see, much to do, and much to remember. Experiencing the full measure of what the city has to offer requires a working knowledge of its history and a healthy dose of organization and planning. This book offers a visual and verbal tour of the sights, sounds, events, peoples, and places that have made, and continue to make, the Alamo City so special. It's the big picture and more. When writing about San Antonio, the most difficult challenge is figuring our where to begin. So, let's start at the top.

From the observation deck atop the 750-foot Tower of the Americas, you truly see San Antonio. On a clear day, the entire city is in view, as is a varied and picturesque countryside, a patchwork of mostly flat farm- and ranchlands to the south and east, gently rolling hills due north, and the fabled Texas Hill Country to the west. Straight down is HemisFair Park, ninety-two acres of redeveloped land that was once the home of HemisFair '68, San Antonio's World's Fair.

This high downtown vantage point gives you the opportunity to not only see, but also feel, the magnificence of a proud place deemed "one of America's four unique cities" by American short-story writer O. Henry. Skyscrapers engulf bricked streets, a shopping mall surrounds a church, the San Antonio River with its legendary cobblestone River Walk meanders through the central city, the Alamo rests in quiet solitude, Market Square brims with activity as people shop and dine, and trollies ding as they travel along. San Antonio is a romantic setting complete with the indelible charm of La Villita (the little village along the river), the elegance of the ageless Menger Hotel, the tranquility of a horse-drawn carriage ride, and a rich past evidenced by the missions of San José, San Juan Capistrano, Concepción, and San Francisco de la Espada. A confluence of cultures makes San Antonio great.

From your cloudlike perch, you'll see the German-influenced King William Historic District, the French architecture of the old Ursuline Academy that is now the Southwest Craft Center, the Spanish character of the Spanish Governor's Palace, and the American-inspired design of the Tower Life Building, a thirty-one-

With five major military installations, San Antonio is the largest military complex in the United States outside of the Washington, D.C., area. Fort Sam Houston is the oldest of the compounds, followed by Kelly, Brooks, Randolph, and Lackland Air Force Bases. Their importance to San Antonio's economy is as impressive as their military history; the military is one of San Antonio's largest industries, second only to tourism.

story Empire State Building look-a-like that was the South's tallest structure when built in the late 1920s. You'll even gaze at river revelers floating on barges, the hustle and bustle of conventioners around the Henry B. Gonzalez Convention Center, an internationally famous zoo, and a spectacular Japanese Tea Garden. From high above the cityscape, pick out Sea World of Texas, the musical theme park Fiesta Texas, five important military installations, and the Alamodome, an indoor sports and meeting complex. You'll also get a bird's-eye view of lush greenbelts and over seventy-five city parks that feature a myriad of tree species including oak, mesquite, cypress, willow, elm, hackberry, mulberry, huisache, persimmon, and pecan. San Antonio's warm, sunbelt climate supports a preponderance of plant life, creating a vivid kaleidoscope of color in the overall beauty of the city below.

Once back on the ground, it's time to immerse yourself in the traditions and passions of the Alamo City. Although the celebration we call "Fiesta San Antonio" is officially in April of each year, San Antonio is really a fiesta everyday. The food alone is enough to get you fired-up. A visit is not complete without Mexican food, margaritas, and mariachis. Bite into a jalapeno, buy a sombrero, barge-in on a river taxi, and be happy. This is San Antonio—alluring and unique. The streets and plazas pulse with excitement. The shops beckon to passers-by. The architecture tastefully blends old and new. Sight-seeing rediscovers days gone by. The experience is exceptional. San Antonio casts a spell.

At one time, the San Antonio Convention and Visitor's Bureau used the promotional theme, "Nowhere else but San Antonio." *En Español es, "Solamente en San Antonio."* The phrase captured the Alamo City's one-of-a-kind nature. Although no longer the official slogan for the city, it still speaks volumes today. Sample a snow cone on the street; find a festival any time of the year; applaud an armadillo race; chase down prize-winning chili with a cold *cerveza;* horse around; or maybe even make a move on the Majestic for a symphony, a Broadway play, or an outstanding individual performance by a nationally known celebrity. San Antonio has something for everyone, at the drop of a hat. But most of all, San Antonio has character. *Solamente en San Antonio* is there a world-famous Hall of Horns. Nowhere else but San Antonio does the social scene range from a cowboy breakfast complete with cowchip tossing to a post-ballet reception with Mikhail Baryshnikov. It's all here. We cherish our past, live our present to the fullest, and anticipate a bright and successful future.

The San Antonio metropolitan area encompasses a population of just over one million people: More than half the inhabitants are of Hispanic descent, about seven percent African-American, a small percentage of Asian and other, and the remainder melting-pot Anglo, affectionately known as "Gringos." We all live together, work together, and enjoy San Antonio together. The city offers a diverse workplace, from manufacturing to military, retail to livestock, tourism to petroleum production, banking to medicine, food processing to steel, and just about everything in between.

The first European visitors came to what is now San Antonio over three hundred years ago. The rest is history. In the pages that follow, you are invited to enjoy an overview of the important people, places, and things that shaped San Antonio.

The Tower of the Americas was the focal point of a spectacular illuminated celebration during the 100th Anniversary of Fiesta in April 1991. Built for HemisFair '68, San Antonio's World's Fair, the Tower is 750 feet tall; diners and sightseers scale the heights in glass-faced elevators located on the outside of the Tower. It's an exhilarating ride, followed by a tremendous view.

Left: The Battle of Flowers Parade, one of the largest parades in America, is the highlight of Fiesta San Antonio. Starting at Broadway and Grayson streets, it winds through just under three miles of downtown streets, thrilling hundreds of thousands of spectators. Brightly colored flowers cover the floats, which carry colorfully dressed participants. ◆ *Above: A guitarist strums a tune at Market Square.*

Significant Dates in San Antonio's Early History

June 1691: San Antonio River discovered and named.

May 1718: First mission (San Antonio de Valero) founded.

February 1720: Mission San José founded.

March 1731: Settlers from the Canary Islands arrive and found Villa San Fernando de Béxar.

March 1731: Three missions (Concepción, San Juan Capistrano, Espada) relocated to San Antonio area from East Texas.

December 1820: Moses Austin arrives in San Antonio to negotiate arrangements for bringing American settlers to New Spain.

September 1824: Mexico wins independence from Spain.

October 1835: Siege of Béxar. Texan forces pitted against Mexican forces holding San Antonio.

December 1835: Ben Milam leads Texans in storming of Béxar (San Antonio). Forces of Mexico under Martín de Perfecto Cos are defeated.

February 23, 1836: Mexican President General Antonio López de Santa Anna arrives with Mexican Army and the thirteen-day siege of the Alamo begins.

March 2, 1836: Texas Declaration of Independence signed at Washington-on-the-Brazos.

March 6, 1836: Alamo falls.

April 21, 1836: Texan forces led by Sam Houston defeat Santa Anna at San Jacinto.

February 1846: Texas annexed by United States.

February 1848: Treaty of Guadalupe Hidalgo ends Mexican War and establishes Rio Grande as southern border of Texas.

February 16, 1861: Committee of local secessionists forces surrender of all United States equipment into its hands.

March 2, 1861: Texas secedes from the Union.

April 1865: Lee surrenders Confederate forces at Appomatox.

June 19, 1865: Major General Gordon Granger of the U.S. Army implements Emancipation Proclamation which frees all slaves in Texas (Juneteenth).

February 1877: The railroad arrives in San Antonio. First train arrives February 19.

December 1879: Fort Sam Houston established.

April 1891: First Battle of Flowers Parade.

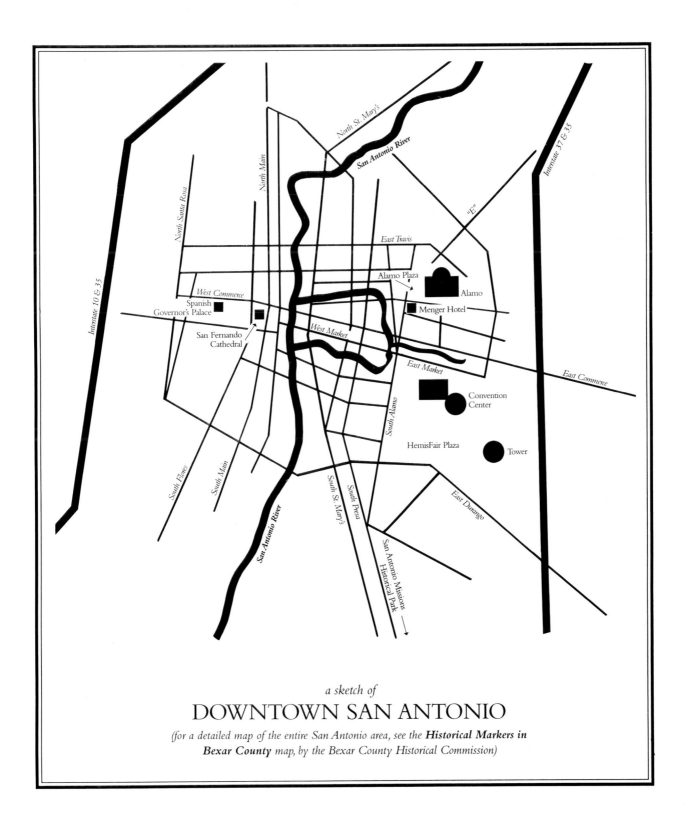

a sketch of

DOWNTOWN SAN ANTONIO

*(for a detailed map of the entire San Antonio area, see the **Historical Markers in Bexar County** map, by the Bexar County Historical Commission)*

Missions

The old Spanish missions of South Texas were constructed by the first European settlers to enter the area—Spaniards arriving by way of Mexico in the early 1700s. The missions were integral to the Spanish blueprint for securing the American Southwest and an important civilizing and economic influence on the raw frontier.

Five of these eighteenth-century missions form a chain that stretches south along the San Antonio River for ten miles. From the Alamo, located in downtown San Antonio and originally known as Mission San Antonio de Valero, to Mission San Francisco de la Espada, lying on the city's southern boundary, the surviving mission structures testify impressively to Spain's attempt to extend its cultural and political hold over the vast areas of New Spain north of the Rio Grande.

Since 1978, four of these missions—Mission Nuestra Señora de la Purisma Concepción de Acuña (Concepción), Mission San José y San Miguel de Aguayo (San José), Mission San Juan Capistrano (San Juan), and Mission San Francisco de la Espada (Espada), along with farmlands that are being acquired as available—have constituted the Spanish Missions National Park. (The fifth mission, known today as the Alamo, is administered by the Daughters of the Republic of Texas.) Rangers are on duty at each location along Mission Trail to answer questions. The Catholic parishes that worship at each of the four mission churches celebrate mass on a regular basis and welcome visitors.

One hundred years ago, a visit to missions Espada and San Juan, ten miles from the city center, meant an overnight trip. Today you can easily explore the four national park missions in a day by following Mission Parkway as it winds south from Mission Concepción to the southernmost mission, Espada. Pick up a map at Concepción or at the San Antonio Missions National Historic Park Headquarters, 2202 Roosevelt Avenue, or hop aboard one of the tour buses leaving from Alamo Plaza.

But first . . . a little history.

While the thirteen colonies on North America's eastern seaboard were gearing up for and fighting the American Revolution, Franciscan priests, Spanish soldier-settlers from northern Mexico, mission Indians,

The elaborate, much-restored facade of the church at Mission San José features statues of San José (Saint Joseph) and the Virgin of Guadalupe, patroness of Mexico. Each of these is flanked by statues of two other saints amid intricate carvings of religious designs and symbols that work together to complete the facade. Magnificent carved cedar doors, replicas of the originals which were stolen in the 1880s, open into a sanctuary of contrasting simplicity and stately beauty.

and a small band of settlers from the Canary Islands were struggling to wrest communities from the sometimes hospitable, often barren and hostile, frontier of New Spain—the area we know today as South Texas.

When Domingo Terán de los Ríos, explorer and first governor of this area, passed through the San Antonio River Valley in 1691 on his way to visit Spain's missions in East Texas, he noted the fine, well-watered country and visualized the valley as an ideal location for a new mission. A community midway between East Texas and the Rio Grande would serve as a convenient stopover for supply caravans traveling to the East Texas missions.

In the late 1600s, Spain's concern that the French, who held Louisiana, might make inroads into New Spain along the Gulf Coast or across the Sabine River had led to the establishment of missions in East Texas. However, it was not until 1718, twenty-seven years after Terán's visit, that the first mission, San Antonio de Valero, was located in the San Antonio area. Mission San José followed in 1720, and in 1731 the remaining three missions (Concepción, San Juan, and Espada) were relocated from East Texas.

Spain had long used the mission system to advance its civilization and to control native peoples while the missionaries converted them to Christianity. The Crown provided funding and protection in the form of forts, or *presidios*. The one or two friars at each mission served not only as spiritual leaders, but also as educators, architectural advisors, contractors, and labor bosses. They recruited the native peoples, converting them to Christianity and teaching them the Spanish language and rules of "civilized" behavior. At the same time priests and natives worked together to design and construct the extensive mission compounds.

The mission Indians came from an aggregate of tribes known as Coahuiltecans, hunter-gatherers who subsisted in the mild South Texas climate on fruits, nuts, beans, seeds, and occasional game and fish. Protection from attack by the Lipan Apaches to the north, as well as the promise of a constant food supply, made mission life attractive to these peaceful peoples.

Though the mission period drew to a close in the early 1800s, the legacy of Spain and the mission Indians can be seen today not only in the historic buildings but also in irrigation practices, ranching equipment and techniques, law, architecture, and language.

The first, or northernmost, mission along Mission Parkway is Nuestra Señora de la Purisma Concepción de Acuña (Mission Concepción), located just east of the confluence of San Pedro Creek and the San Antonio River. A map will show you that the Spanish padres were mindful of the availability of water for both the mission compounds and the outlying fields. However, trial and error, as well as common sense and luck, were required to avoid settling in the flood plain. Both San Antonio de Valero and San José missions were moved several times before safe locations were secured.

When you arrive at Mission Concepción, you'll notice the distinctive triangle above the door matched by pyramid shapes atop each bell tower. The geometric simplicity of this facade was originally enlivened by painted quatrefoils and squares of red, blue, and yellow—Moorish designs thought to appeal to the Indians. The colors remained vivid as late as 1890, but have since weathered to faint traces.

The mission compound at Concepción is no longer in existence, but the church itself looks much as it did two hundred years ago. Constructed of adobe and a light, porous limestone quarried nearby, it is thought to be the oldest unrestored and still intact church in America. Fortunately, it survived its stint as a troop barracks and as a cattle pen in the mid-1800s.

The interior follows the traditional European cathedral design—a vaulted cruciform shape with baptistry and bell room on either side of the entrance door and a dome topped by a small cupola above the intersection of the arms of the cruciform. The small, vaulted chapels, located at the base of each bell tower, were once covered with splendid murals though only patchy fragments remain. Many find this church to be the most beautifully proportioned of all the mission churches. The nave is noted for its fine acoustics.

Continue along Mission Parkway for about three miles. The next mission you'll encounter is San José y San Miguel de Aguayo, established in 1720 by Father Antonio Margil, a priest from the East Texas missions who found the San Antonio area to his liking and petitioned the authorities in Mexico for permission to relocate.

The most extensively renovated of all the sites, San José with its careful restorations will provide you with a window into the order, security, and austere

The seventy-five-foot bell tower of the San José Church, rebuilt after its collapse in 1930, rises above the tree line just off Mission Road. The rounded shape at the bottom of the photo contains a circular stairway leading to the bell tower and choir loft. The hand-hewn steps of the spiral staircase are held together without nails or pegs; in the 1920s, these solid oak blocks were found scattered about the grounds and were carefully restored and reassembled to their original condition.

Left: The intricate rose window, as well as much of the work on the facade of San José, have been attributed to Pedro Huizar, a talented young stonecarver who lived at the mission with his wife and family in the 1700s. The design of the rose window appears now and again around San Antonio, most notably outlining the display windows at the Rivercenter Dillards Department Store and providing the shape for a lily pond at the McNay Art Museum. ♦ Above: Afternoon sunlight illuminates a statue of the Virgin Mary to the left of the main altar in San José Church.

The interior of Mission San José has been completely rebuilt. A photo from the turn of the twentieth century shows the sanctuary open to the sky with only the sacristy and bell tower remaining. Fortunately, the Conservation Society took an active interest in the mission and began, in 1924, to generate the funds, interest, and effort required to preserve the site for future generations.

beauty the padres sought to create from the bountiful but chaotic wilderness.

A fine diorama in the granary at San José takes you through a typical mission day, giving a sense of the endless work required to operate a mission and an appreciation for the management skills required of the friars and overseers. Daily chores were governed by routines as predictable and symmetrical as the mission architecture. Rations were issued on certain days, and the passage of the day itself was marked by the ringing of mission bells to signal changes of activity from dawn to nightfall.

San José's thick stone walls, reinforced on the interior by the workshops and living quarters, enclose a perfectly square compound 611 feet on each side, with facilities serving all the needs of the community—workshops for weavers, carpenters, and blacksmiths; a sugar mill for making cane syrup and brown sugar bars; a water supply; storage facilities; a granary; and a convent with offices for the priests.

The church itself, with its carved stonework and wooden doors, simple but beautiful interior, and solid oak circular stairway to the bell tower, is a monument to artisanship and ingenuity. A visiting priest in the eighteenth century, Friar Morfi, wrote, "This building, because of its size, good taste, and beauty, would grace a large city as a parish church."

In addition to the enclosed compounds and surrounding fields, each mission operated a livestock-raising facility some miles distant. The San José ranch, El Atascosa, was located to the south of San José. At times it ran as many as three thousand head each of cattle and sheep, one hundred horses for *vaqueros* and shepherds, eighty mares, and thirty yoke of oxen.

When Friar Gaspar José Solís stopped at Rancho del Atascosa in 1768, he wrote that the ranch was entirely operated by mission Indians with no Spanish overseer—testimony to the innate abilities of the native Cohuiltecans and the training and organizational skills of the priests, as well as to the scarcity of priests and soldiers. Though the use of horses in New Spain remained the exclusive privilege of the Spanish *cabelleros,* the gentlemen of the Spanish haciendas, this rule was overlooked on the frontier. For the native *vaquero,* forerunner of the American cowboy, the horse was the mainstay of daily work.

About a mile down the parkway from Mission San José, you'll come to Espada Park and the oldest existing dam in the United States. Espada Dam is of interest from an engineering standpoint because, unlike in most dams, the walls curve downstream with the flow of the water. Nevertheless, it has lasted over two hundred years. Due to flood control measures taken in the 1950s, the main river channel now bypasses Espada Dam. The dam and its water level, however, have been carefully preserved.

With the unpredictable rainfall and hot, dry summers of South Texas, the mission irrigation systems received high priority. Based on the *acequia*—a Spanish word from the Arabic *as-sāqiyah* meaning "irrigation stream"—the system, originally developed by the Moors for the arid regions of Spain, was easily adapted to the American Southwest and served to insure a plentiful supply of water and food.

One of the earliest examples of planned water use in North America, *acequias* were employed by the *villa* (town) and *presidio* (fort) as well; at one time seven *acequias* drew from the waters of San Pedro Creek and the San Antonio River. Strict rules prohibited the use of irrigation ditches for laundry or trash disposal. This fifteen-mile network, which included five dams and at least two aqueducts, irrigated nearly 3,500 acres of land.

The Espada system, including Espada Aqueduct which carries the *acequia* waters over Piedras Creek, still flows today and is considered the oldest irrigation system in the United States.

The last two missions along the trail, San Juan Capistrano and San Francisco de la Espada, appear small in comparison to San José and have not undergone such extensive renovation. However, San Juan at one time yielded massive quantities of produce—enough to support not only itself but also other local missions, the *presidio,* and town, as well as an established trade route to Louisiana and Mexico.

Distinctive belfries at both San Juan and Espada consist of triple arches piercing the flat wall above the chapel doors, each arch designed to hold a bell.

The altar in the chapel at San Juan is flanked by very old statues of Christ and the Virgin Mary. Made of cornstalk pith and coated and painted, they are products of a process perfected by the Indians of central Mexico before the Spanish Conquest. The central figure above the altar is that of San Juan Capistrano, a fifteenth-century theologian for whom the mission was named. Dressed in the armor of the

History indicates that the chapel at Mission San Juan Capistrano was to have been replaced by a larger, grander church. However, only the foundation of this replacement remains—across the quadrangle from the chapel.

Each Sunday at Mission San José, a group of mariachi musicians assists in celebrating the noon mass. Following the service, the congregation follows the mariachis to an area behind the church where young dancers in traditional dress perform for parishioners and visitors.

crusades, he rests his right foot on a turbaned human head.

Noteworthy today at Espada is the chapel (rebuilt in 1868) with its unusual Moorish door. Observe that the stones at the base of the arch have been reversed, causing a break in the line of the arch. Whether this unusual configuration occurred by accident or design is unknown.

Espada, in danger of disappearing completely during the 1800s, was rescued by a twenty-nine-year-old Franciscan, Father François Bouchu, who was so attracted to this, the most remote of missions, that he took up residence in 1858. For the next forty years, he personally restored much of the old mission, rebuilding the church and adding a wood floor, choir loft, sanctuary railing, and pews. Bouchu is said to have worked on the restoration until a week before his death.

After leaving Mission Espada, follow Espada Road for a mile and a half, looking carefully for historical markers, and see the Espada Aqueduct. Built of a soft and easily quarried limestone that hardens with exposure to air, the Roman arches of the 250-year-old aqueduct support a channel four feet wide and four feet deep that carries irrigation water over Piedras Creek.

The mission system waxed and waned throughout the eighteenth century. The health of the mission Indians was never strong. Measles, cholera, smallpox, and typhoid devastated the Indian population, which had no resistance to these European diseases. Many tired of the restrictive community life and simply walked away. The Lipan Apaches found the fledgling *villas* and the Indians working outside the mission walls easy marks for attack. For all these reasons, a thriving second generation of mission In-

Left: The setting sun pierces the belfry of San Juan Capistrano, outlining the delicate bell tower which has withstood the ravages of time for more than two hundred years. The bell towers at Missions San Juan and Espada bear a striking similarity to each other, although close scrutiny reveals differences in detail and materials.
◆ *Above: Espada Aqueduct, constructed by the Spanish missionaries sometime between 1731 and 1745 to carry the* acequia *water over Piedras Creek, continues to function today, making it a part of the oldest irrigation system in the United States.*

dians never materialized, and new workers had to be continually recruited.

Finally, toward the end of the 1700s the Spanish government turned to defending itself against revolution from within and began to abandon the missions. In addition, it imposed a tax on mission cattle, which destroyed this means of livelihood. By 1821 Mexico had won its independence from Spain, and by 1824 all the missions had become secular communities. Although some sections of San Juan were rented to Spanish colonists, most mission land, livestock, and movable inventory were parceled out to the remaining Indians.

The mission communities, designed initially to be self-sufficient and totally separate from the *villa* and the *presidio,* now merged with those populations. By the turn of the century, the community centered between San Pedro Creek and the San Antonio River had become an amalgam of Canary Islanders, mission Indians, and residents from the *presidio.*

The buildings themselves began to crumble. Visitors in 1890, one hundred years after secularization, could send their friends a postcard showing the weed-covered ruins of San José with the inscription "The Mission, between the elements and the festive vandal, will soon be no more."

Today, thanks to Los Compadres (Friends of the Missions), the San Antonio Conservation Society, the National Park Service, the Diocese of San Antonio, and the parish communities, as well as the many individuals in San Antonio who care about the preservation of the missions, the San Antonio missions have not succumbed to the "elements and the festive vandal." Instead, they stand as centerpieces of the history of San Antonio and the Southwest.

Mission Espada, formally known as San Francisco de la Espada — Saint Francis of the Sword — is one of the three missions relocated from East Texas in 1731. Upon relocation "Espada" was added to the name for reasons unknown today, though some believe that the upraised hand of the altar figure of Saint Francis at one time held an espada, *or sword.*

The intimate chapel of Mission Espada was one of the first San Antonio missions to be built of stone—and the first to collapse. According to author Charles Ramsdell, it was complete and in use by 1756, but by 1758 the roof had fallen in. Only the front and back walls remained. However, a French priest, Father Bouchu, took it upon himself to restore the mission, spending forty years on the project. The chapel was rebuilt around 1868.

Above: Detail of a bell in the pierced three-bell tower at Mission Espada. ♦ Right: The exterior of Mission Concepción Church has changed little in two hundred years. To the right of the church is an arched walkway with rooms that may have been living quarters for the priests.

The Alamo

Known worldwide as "the cradle of Texas liberty," the Alamo, to the surprise of first-time visitors, nestles quietly in downtown San Antonio, its walled gardens a pleasant respite from the turmoil of city life that swirls around it.

Scale models inside the Alamo chapel show that much of the famous battle, in which more than 180 Texans and Americans suffered defeat and death at the hands of the army of Antonio López de Santa Anna in March of 1836, took place between the church and South Alamo Street where Alamo Plaza lies today. You can see a part of the original west wall of the Alamo grounds as you enter the Paseo del Alamo, which leads from Alamo Plaza to the River Walk.

The Alamo is best known, of course, as the site of the bloody battle between Mexicans and Texas settlers, but it began its existence as the first Spanish mission in the San Antonio River Valley. Officially founded in 1718, Mission San Antonio de Valero was not settled in its present location until six years later. Historians suspect that the first location lay to the west of San Pedro Creek near the present-day intersection of North Salado and Laredo streets.

A year after the founding, Father Antonio Olivares, the first priest of the mission, moved it just east of the River Bend, about where Saint Joseph's Church stands today. But in 1724, a hurricane destroyed the huts and small stone tower at the second location, and Mission San Antonio de Valero was moved to its final resting place a bit to the north.

Standing in front of the Alamo today, you are hardly aware of the river that passes just a few hundred yards to the west. Yet the river was probably the most important feature of the landscape when Father Olivares chose this location. A desirable site had to be close to water but not prone to flooding. Surrounding fields must be easily irrigated in order to support the mission's agricultural endeavors.

Though the river was nearby, the first task of the mission Indians recruited by Father Olivares was to construct the Alamo Madre Ditch, a two-and-a-half-mile *acequia* that carried water for irrigation and drinking from the headwaters of the river—near present-day Incarnate Word College at Broadway and Hildebrand

The familiar facade of the Alamo had a markedly different appearance in 1836 when the famous battle occurred. At that time it was complete only to the cornices. The rounded, upper part, designed by architect John Fries, along with a roof and two interior support pillars, were added by the United States Army after they leased the building in 1849 for use as a quartermaster depot. Statuary niches on either side of the door were a part of the original church design.

Avenue—south behind the mission walls and back into the river in the King William area.

In addition to the water system, the mission Indians constructed living quarters, offices for the priests, kitchens, and a dining hall. The *convento,* a part of which later became the Long Barrack (where many Texans and Americans died in the Battle of the Alamo), was originally a two-story building with arches on both floors. It was arranged in a square with an interior courtyard.

Records indicate that the church itself, begun in 1744, collapsed twice. The original plan probably called for two bell towers, but the builders only completed the facade (which carries the date of 1758) up to the cornices.

Though inspectors described Mission San Antonio de Valero as a thriving community in the mid-1770s, by 1793 the Indian population was in serious decline. Mission San Antonio became the first of the five missions to undergo secularization. The government distributed the rich farmlands to the Indians and shut down the mission. By the time of the Texas Revolution (War of Independence) in 1835–36, many involved had no inkling that their fort had once existed as a religious community.

The Spanish authorities stationed troops from the Mexican town of San Jose y Santiago del Alamo de Parras at Mission San Antonio de Valero for twelve years beginning in 1801. The garrison's hometown, Alamo ("cottonwood") de Parras, was so named because of its proximity to a certain cottonwood tree in Coahuila, Mexico. In San Antonio, the name of the garrison was commonly shortened to El Alamo, and over time the troops' quarters themselves became known as El Alamo. Thus Mission San Antonio de Valero acquired the name that survives into the twentieth century.

After gaining independence from Spain in 1821, the Mexican government continued to encourage immigration from the United States and Europe as a means of populating what it called the Northern Frontier. Throughout the 1820s, Anglo-Americans joined Stephen F. Austin and other *empresarios,* "land agents," who, by permission of the Mexican government, controlled the settlement of vast quantities of land; other Anglos simply slipped in unnoticed and claimed a bit of Texas for themselves. In exchange for land, settlers agreed to accept the Mexican constitution and the doctrines of the Roman Catholic Church.

By 1830, the Mexican government had become concerned about the burgeoning numbers of immigrants from the north. Though they had hoped to encourage Europeans and Mexicans to colonize the area, the vast majority were Anglos and their African-American slaves from the American South. These newer Anglos did not assimilate into the Mexican culture as early Anglo immigrants had; instead, they formed their own enclaves, speaking English and retaining their Anglo customs.

In an attempt to counter these trends, Mexico passed a law in 1830 prohibiting further immigration to Mexico from the United States. Earlier it had begun rescinding tax abatements formerly used to encourage immigration to the Northern Frontier. The new law, piled on top of these previous mandates, alarmed settlers, who felt that their land claims were in jeopardy and worried that a highly centralized Mexican government might enforce an 1829 law abolishing slavery.

When Santa Anna became president of Mexico, the movement toward a strong central government seemed unavoidable. Nevertheless, settlers remained divided between those who advocated pressuring the Mexican government to return to the more favorable Constitution of 1824 and those who leaned toward independence from Mexico. Many Tejanos (Texans of Spanish-Indian ancestry) in San Antonio were dissatisfied with Mexican rule and in the end sided with the Anglo-Americans against Santa Anna, even though this path led to their becoming minority citizens in their own land.

Tensions heightened, and in 1835 Santa Anna sent his brother-in-law, General Martín Perfecto de Cos, to secure San Antonio. All that autumn, the Texans laid siege to San Antonio where General Cos and his eight hundred men were encamped. Cos tore down the arches of the Alamo church on the east side and constructed an earthen ramp so that his soldiers could haul cannons to the top of the wall.

Despite Cos's preparations at the Alamo, the final hours of the Siege of Béxar took place not around the fort, but in the streets, plazas, and homes across the river to the west. Ben Milam, former Indian fighter and scout, led the Texan army in five days of hand-to-hand combat against Cos and his forces. Milam himself was one of the four Texans killed that December.

The Paseo del Alamo was constructed in 1981 to open a passageway from Alamo Plaza through the Hyatt Hotel to the main bend of the San Antonio River. During excavation part of the original west wall of the Alamo was uncovered and can be seen at the entrance to the waterfall-lined walkway.

The defeated Cos signed the surrender papers in a house in La Villita, now known as the Cos House. Enraged by this defeat of the Mexican forces, Santa Anna vowed to eradicate resistance in San Antonio, which at this time consisted of fewer than two thousand citizens.

In late February of 1836, Santa Anna and his four thousand troops attacked. Although the Texan forces received word that the Mexican Army had crossed the Rio Grande with a large force, they did not expect Santa Anna to cover the intervening brushland so quickly.

The Texans fortified the Alamo as best they could, using the earthen mounds and cannons left behind by Cos in the earlier siege. The compound was difficult to guard, however, with only 150 men available to defend the four acres. On the morning of February 23, William Travis and James Bowie, joint commanders, moved all their forces to the Alamo compound. Santa Anna entered the city unimpeded, flying the red flag of no quarter from the tower of San Fernando Church on Main Plaza. The Texans answered his demand for surrender with a shot from the Alamo.

On February 24, Travis wrote his famous letter, addressed to the "People of Texas and all Americans in the World," in which he vowed to fight to the death. His request for reinforcements went largely unanswered, with the exception of thirty-two men from Gonzales, a town to the east, who offered their services, entering the compound on March 1.

Couriers continued to leave and reenter the Alamo with relative ease, and it appears that the defenders could have effected a nighttime escape many times during the siege. But, though the odds were clearly against them, the soldiers, almost to a man, chose to stay and fight.

The final assault occurred at dawn on March 6 — thirteen days after the beginning of the siege; it lasted less than two hours. All the defenders were killed. A few women and children who had taken refuge in the Alamo survived. Santa Anna gave each two dollars and a blanket and let them go to spread word of the massacre to their fellow Texans.

The Mexicans ordered the bodies of the defenders burned, according to the account of Fran-

The Menger Hotel opened its doors on Alamo Plaza in 1859 to serve the commercial district growing up around the Army's Quartermaster Depot located in the old Alamo. Its history includes such famous guests as General Robert E. Lee, poet Sidney Lanier, writer O. Henry, and of course, Teddy Roosevelt, who is said to have recruited his "Rough Riders" in the famous Menger Bar.

cisco Antonio Ruiz who, along with other officials of the city, was commanded to build the enormous pyre and assist in transporting the Mexican dead to their burial ground in a cemetery near today's Santa Rosa Hospital. Ruiz reported that the "gallantry of the few Texians who defended the Alamo was really wondered at by the Mexican army. Even the generals were astonished at their vigorous resistance and how dearly victory had been bought."

Indeed Santa Anna had lost hundreds of men to the Alamo's 182 defenders. Many more of the Mexican army were incapacitated by wounds. The time it took them to regroup and move out of San Antonio gave Sam Houston and the forces of the newly created Republic of Texas time to prepare for battle. On April 21 at San Jacinto, not far from present-day Houston, the tables were turned. The Texan forces surprised and overwhelmed Santa Anna's army in a brief but decisive battle.

The Alamo lay in ruins for over ten years after the battle. Then, in 1849, the United States Army leased it from the Roman Catholic Church as a quartermaster depot for the storage of hay and grain. The army repaired the fort, raised the walls of the church and convent, and added a roof and two windows to the facade. At this time, the characteristic upper portion of the Alamo facade was designed and added—providing the familiar arched shape that crops up unexpectedly all over San Antonio. The army used the chapel as a depot until 1878, when it opened the new Government Hill site, today's Fort Sam Houston.

After serving as a mission, a fort, and a storage depot, the Alamo played a new role in the community in 1878—that of shopping emporium. Honoré Grenet, a merchant of French descent, leased all the grounds except the chapel at a price of $19,000 for ninety-nine years. He built a fortlike structure on top of the barracks and convent, turning them into a department store containing an "ocean of goods of every imaginable description." The Alamo Church became his warehouse. When Grenet died in 1882, Hugo and Schmeltzer, wholesale grocers and liquor dealers, acquired the lease from Grenet's estate and continued to use the old mission for retail purposes.

The chapel itself was sold in 1883 to the state of Texas for $20,000; the state cleaned it out, repaired the roof, and gave custody to the city of San Antonio. The Daughters of the Republic of Texas (DRT)—

many of whom are descendants of Alamo defenders—organized in 1891, with one of their objectives the preservation of historic sites. This group intervened in 1903 to prevent a syndicate from turning the Hugo and Schmeltzer site into a hotel. By 1905, the state of Texas had purchased the barracks and the grounds and turned custody over to the DRT, which has since maintained and operated the entire Alamo compound at no cost to the taxpayers of Texas.

Meanwhile, the plaza in front of the old Alamo chapel developed into a center of city life. In 1859, German brewer William Menger opened his elegant hotel on the southeast corner of the plaza, and later, when the San Antonio Street Railway System began to carry passengers from Alamo Plaza to the lush picnic and amusement park at San Pedro Springs in 1878, much of downtown commercial and outdoor market activity centered around the plaza.

Though the plaza has been arranged and rearranged over the years, the basic configuration has remained the same, with streets and landscaped park occupying what was once the mission's courtyard.

The grounds of the Alamo include a number of newer buildings designed to blend in with the older historic structures. The proceeds of the DRT's museum and souvenir shop support the upkeep of the Alamo compound. The DRT also maintains an extensive research library and meeting hall.

For visitors and newcomers interested in a comprehensive overview of San Antonio's history, the exhibits and slide show available in the Long Barrack at the Alamo are an excellent place to begin.

The Alamo chapel contains additional exhibits showing details of the battle. You can also see the reconstructed rooms where the defenders made their last stand, along with a collection of memorabilia from the Battle of the Alamo and from the men who fought there. Included are such items as Davy Crockett's buckskin vest and rifle, the Bowie family knife, Travis's estate records, flintlock rifles, maps, and paintings.

Like the scant remains of Mission San Antonio de Valero, these items can never tell us the whole story of the mission-fort, but they bear witness to its long and varied past. The intimate details from the lives of the defenders and their families and from the Alamo itself stand as a symbol of those ideals that call for the ultimate sacrifice.

The cenotaph, with relief figures of the defenders of the Alamo sculpted by local artist Pompeo Coppini, was erected on Alamo Plaza in 1936 to commemorate the one-hundred-year anniversary of the Battle of the Alamo. Names of the defenders are chiseled into the base, and statues of James Bonham, James Bowie, Davy Crockett, and William Travis are located on each side. The Emily Morgan Hotel can be seen in the background to the right.

In the stillness of early morning, you can almost hear the echo of cannons at the Alamo grounds.

The River Walk

"I know that river, it's my baby. They used to call me Old Man River." These words of Robert H. H. Hugman, concept architect of the San Antonio River Walk, were printed in the San Antonio *Light* on May 19, 1974. He was right. The San Antonio River was his baby, and the River Walk, as we know it today, was his vision, his dream.

The story of the development of the San Antonio River Walk began with a natural disaster. In September 1921, the city experienced a severe flood. Heavy rains caused the San Antonio River to overflow its banks and completely cover large portions of the downtown sector. In some places, flood waters measured eight to nine feet above street level. Lives were lost, and citizens were justifiably outraged. City of San Antonio government officials had no choice but to face the problem head-on. Hawley and Freese, an engineering firm, was hired to study the situation and make recommendations. Two of their suggestions were approved and enacted, but two were not. One of the rejected ideas called for the river area we now refer to as the Paseo del Rio, or River Walk, to be converted into a thoroughfare. History tells us that losing the river did not appeal to the San Antonio Conservation Society and the City Federation of Women's Clubs. Not only did they stop this proposal, but suggested the river and its banks be preserved and transformed into a city park. Robert Hugman shared their view.

Robert H. H. Hugman, a native San Antonian, graduated in June 1924 from the School of Architecture and Design at the University of Texas in Austin. He spent the next three years living and working in New Orleans, where he witnessed the ongoing conservation and preservation program painstakingly administered in the Vieux Carré district. Upon returning to San Antonio in the spring of 1927, Hugman envisioned the same kind of effort being afforded the San Antonio River. His objectives were to save the natural beauty of the setting; control flooding; add pedestrian walkways on both sides of the river; construct appropriate bridges and walkways over the waterway; and develop shops, restaurants, cabarets, clubs, an outdoor theater, hotels, and apartments along its banks.

To take his vision from drawing board to reality, Hugman met with the mayor, two city commissioners,

Trees along the River Walk are decorated with multicolored lights during the holiday season; the Lighting of the Lights ceremony takes place on the evening of the day after Thanksgiving every year. The Hilton Palacio del Rio Hotel, in the background, was the first modularly constructed building in the world. The modular concept was created by the H. B. Zachry Co. in order to have the hotel ready for the opening of HemisFair '68—start-to-finish erection time was approximately 250 days. Each of the hotel's rooms were built and furnished at the Zachry "room factory" on the south side of San Antonio, and then shipped to the site, lifted to the proper floor, and blown into position using a giant helicopter blade fan.

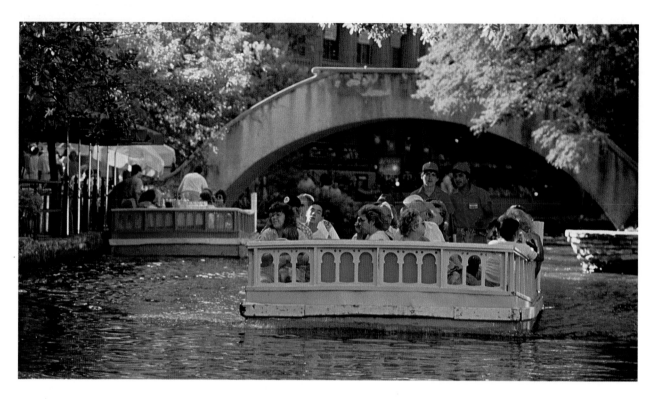

Just as in River Walk concept architect Robert H. H. Hugman's vision, a barge passes by a sidewalk cafe on the San Antonio River. Each day thousands of visitors cross from one bank to the other on the arched stone bridge.

property owners, and civic leaders on June 28, 1929. He spoke eloquently of his plan to turn the San Antonio River into a graceful, romantic, and historic centerpiece for the city. He evoked images of the shop-lined cobblestone streets in Spain and the gondola-plied waterways in Venice. His ideas met with favorable reaction, but the Great Depression made funding of the project virtually impossible. Undaunted, Robert Hugman continued to promote the idea of river beautification at every opportunity.

Finally on October 25, 1938, the city of San Antonio issued a $75,000 bond, endorsed by seventy-four of the seventy-six property owners and residents who owned or lived on property on either side of the river from Jefferson to Villita streets. Issuance of the bond opened the flood gates, so to speak, for securing a $355,000 federal grant through the Works Progress Administration (WPA). After almost ten years of living the dream, Hugman was officially hired as architect of the San Antonio River Beautification Project. What stands today as the San Antonio River Walk basically reflects Robert Hugman's original concept and design. Sadly, after only seventeen months on the job, Hugman was relieved of his duties. As the story

goes, he was informed by WPA bookkeepers that materials designated for use on the River Walk had been delivered and used at another project in the city. Hugman took the evidence provided to him by WPA personnel to a well-known city judge who was a member of the River Board. Almost immediately, he was fired. In doing right, he was wronged. The project was completed without him on March 14, 1941.

Today, the San Antonio River Walk is the graceful, romantic, historic centerpiece of Robert Hugman's dreams. The charm created by cobblestone walkways along an emerald green stream is real. It can be felt. Artful landscaping provides a lasting legacy. The shops are all in place, similar to those in the original drawings. Sidewalk cafés and cabarets line the riverbanks. Hotels and apartments rise toward the sky. The music of mariachis fills the air. River barges represent gondolas. The Arneson River Theatre is there too.

Ernie Pyle, the well-known journalist of the 1940s, once described the San Antonio River Walk as "the American Venice," but an anonymous passerby may have said it best: "The River Walk is San Antonio."

In this city of celebrations, a gathering of people enjoying food and festivities right along the river is a common sight.

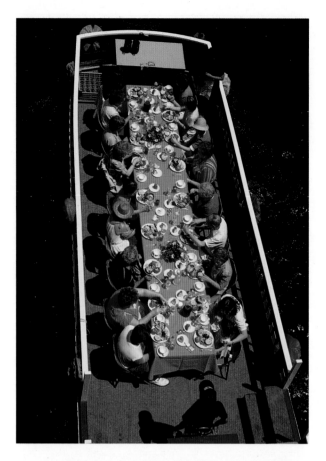

◆ *Above: Many restaurants on the River Walk arrange for private barge dining excursions. It's a treat worth trying!* ◆ *Left: Since its original completion, the San Antonio River Walk has undergone two major additions. You would never know by looking, but the river was lengthened to reach the area in front of the Henry B. Gonzalez Convention Center just prior to HemisFair '68, and then diverted again to encompass the Rivercenter area. Rivercenter, a large and spectacular downtown shopping mall, is shown here.*

Visitors and locals alike enjoy a barge ride on the river. It's an inexpensive way to see the sights and beauty of the River Walk, and it offers an historical perspective of the city. The ride takes just less than an hour and winds its way on emerald green water below the downtown street level.

Neighborhoods & Architecture

San Antonio's rich architectural heritage has been crafted over the years by its many citizens—missionaries, Indians, Spanish and Mexican pioneers, settlers from the United States, and emigrants from all over the world. But, you must look beyond the Alamo and the River Walk to capture the essence of this layered, thriving city with its long-reaching roots and diverse styles.

As you travel about San Antonio, observe the many striking architectural forms working together to create a symphony of angle and light. Some buildings have little surviving history, no one to tell the tale of their origins; only details of design that link them to one period or another; others come with full pedigree, but all stand to help us understand the life patterns upon which our city is built.

Early San Antonio consisted of three independent, rival communities. In addition to the missions, two other groups established themselves in the San Antonio River Valley in the 1700s—the soldier-settlers of the *presidio* ("fort") and a small band from the Canary Islands who founded Villa San Fernando in 1731.

The Presidio de San Antonio de Béxar was organized in 1718, at the same time as Mission San Antonio de Valero. The mission was named Valero for the Viceroy of Mexico, while "Bexar" honored the Viceroy's brother, the Duke de Béjar or Béxar (pronounced "bear"). In later years as the communities along the San Antonio River grew and merged, Bexar came to describe the whole area around the headwaters of the river, and still later the county surrounding San Antonio became Bexar County.

The *presidio* was established to protect and assist the missions and served as fort and home to the Spanish soldiers and their families. Recruited from the northern regions of Mexico (Coahuila, Saltillo, and Nuevo Leon) to maintain the *presidio,* these frontierspeople were already accustomed to the hardships and isolation of wilderness existence.

The permanent location of the Spanish *presidio* was determined in 1722 by the Marqués de San Miguel de Aguayo, the energetic and farsighted governor of Coahuila and Texas. He moved the *presidio* to a flat, fertile strip of land between San Pedro Creek and the big bend of the San Antonio River, both of which flowed vigorously in those days. The rivers provided irrigation as well as a natural line of defense against Indian

The Spanish Governor's Palace contained both public and private rooms. This family living room, located just behind the formal entrance area, opens to the bedrooms and to a semi-enclosed patio just before the main garden. Floors are of huge flagstones; the ceiling beams are hand-hewn. Walls three feet thick and a deep roof of earth and gravel together with the wood-burning fireplace insulated the occupants from heat and cold.

attack. And the fields enclosed by the horseshoe bend of the San Antonio River afforded a rich and protected pasture for the garrison's horses; Commerce Street, which later bisected these fields, was known for some time known as El Potrero, or the Horse Pasture.

A garrison of sorts was built with its west wall running along San Pedro Creek. In addition to defending the mission, the soldiers cleared land, opened *acequias* to irrigate the fields, planted crops, and built *jacals* (small dwellings consisting of walls of upright wooden poles chinked with mud or clay and roofs of thatch) for themselves and their families. The community that formed around the *presidio* consisted, in 1726, of over fifty presidial families with a total of more than two hundred inhabitants. As soldiers left military service many settled in the Villa San Fernando as civilians.

The year 1731 was one of upheaval for these two emergent communities of the San Antonio River Valley. On March 5, Missions Concepción, San Juan, and Espada moved into the area, relocating from East Texas. Four days later, a weary band of fifty-six persons arrived at Presidio de Bexar, having traveled from the Canary Islands under the auspices of the Spanish government for the purpose of becoming permanent settlers in New Spain. Expecting an established farming community, the Canary Islanders were shocked to find raw frontier with much of the desirable land already laid claim to by the missions and the *presidio* dwellers. Open land to the west and north of town would remain under the control of hostile Apaches for years to come.

The *presidio* and Missions San Antonio de Valero and San José had by then been in existence for over ten years. Engrossed in meeting daily requirements for food, shelter, and defense, the families of the *presidio* had made no personal legal claim to their lands. When the Canary Islanders arrived armed with promises from the King of Spain and orders for the captain of the *presidio* about land distribution, the soldier-settlers suddenly found themselves divested of their irrigated fields and water rights. The *Isleños* ("Islanders"), as they came to be known, also received a square of land between the *presidio* and the bend of the river. This square became their town and was named Villa San Fernando after the heir to the Spanish throne.

The three groups—missions, Canary Islanders, *presidio* dwellers—attempted to remain separate and independent. Each competed with the others for water, farmlands, and grazing rights. None encouraged marriage outside the group. But by the end of the eighteenth century, economic and social necessity together with intermarriage had brought Canary Islanders, Mestizos, Indians, and Spanish together into one identifiable Tejano community of about two thousand souls. Community status began to be determined less by origins and more by economic success. Unfortunately, except for the missions, few structures from the 1700s survive today. The buildings of Villa San Fernando may be long gone, but the basic blueprint of modern San Antonio dates back to those first Spanish settlers. A map from the 1700s depicts the important features of San Antonio; then, as now, Plaza de Armas (Military Plaza), Plaza de las Islas (Main Plaza), the U-shaped river bend, and Mission San Antonio de Valero (the Alamo) formed the underpinnings of the communities evolving between the two rivers.

In early San Antonio, the principal citizens lived around the plazas or within one or two blocks of them. These plazas were modeled after those of European cities, intended to contain fountains and activity centers and to function as the community gathering grounds. The plazas remained the focus of city life until the turn of the century brought the electric tram, the automobile, and the consequent flight to suburbia. Though downtown was no longer a residential area, the location of the City Hall in the middle of Military Plaza, the Bexar County Courthouse on the south side of Main Plaza, the rescue of the Alamo in 1906, and the revitalization of the river in the 1930s insured the perpetuation of the original configuration.

After the Texas Revolution, emigrants from the United States and Europe, particularly Germany, began to arrive in San Antonio in substantial numbers; Anglo travelers in the mid-1800s wrote of how the styles of Europe, the Southern Plantation, and New England were gradually replacing the Spanish character of the architecture. Flat roofs and adobe walls were giving way to two-story houses with pitched roofs and columned verandas. Front yards were taking the place of central courtyards.

The Spanish Governor's Palace, located on the west side of Plaza de Armas (Military Plaza), is the one remaining structure from the original Presidio de San Antonio de Béxar. Completed in 1749 and

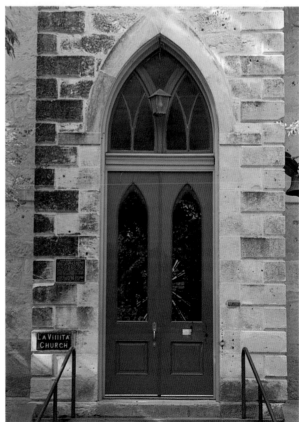

Above: The simple exterior of the Spanish Governor's Palace, San Antonio's one remaining Spanish Colonial home, belies the elegance of the interior. Built in the mid-1700s, the Palace contains ten rooms and a small loft with an extensive walled garden in the rear. The flags of France, Spain, Mexico, the Republic of Texas, the Confederacy, and the United States that fly in front of the Palace represent the six sovereignties that have laid claim to Texas since the seventeenth century. ◆ Right: The quaint La Villita Church lies in the heart of an historic district bordered by Alamo, South Presa, Villita, and Nueva streets. La Villita, or "Little Village," features both European and Mexican styles of architecture.

used as a residence and office by the presidial captain (never the official residence of the governor), this gracious but simple building, with its flat roof, flagstone floors, arches, and walled garden, was restored to its original floor plan in 1929 after years of use as a school, bar, and tailor shop.

Plaza de Armas served as a military post, stockyard, and drill ground from 1722 until the advent of the Republic of Texas in 1836. From then on, as English place names were substituted for the customary Spanish, it became known as Military Plaza. In the 1840s it was cleared of buildings and transformed into a municipal market and open-air restaurant.

Stephen Gould's 1882 *Alamo City Guide* advised visitors to "proceed at once to Military Plaza and see the Plaza Market, one of the distinctive features of San Antonio." Early photos capture a square teeming with village activity—wagon trains, chili stands, hay wagons, produce vendors, and customers milling everywhere. Vendors sold vegetables, eggs, butter, poultry, chili peppers, and even songbirds in wicker cages.

By the 1880s, the "chili queens" had become an integral part of plaza life. According to Frank Tolbert in *A Bowl of Red,* these young women arrived on the south side of the plaza at dusk, bringing tables, charcoal braziers, and their cooked chili in clay pots. They set up oilcloth-covered tables and stools for customers. A large ornate lamp with colorful globe lit each table, and all night the pungent aroma of chili simmering over mesquite coals called plaza residents, wagon drivers, locals, and visitors to a feast.

According to Tolbert and others, chili may well have originated in San Antonio, evolving from a dish invented by poor families to stretch small portions of costly meat into as many servings as possible. In any event, the chili queens continued to vend chili on one plaza or another until the 1940s when health department regulations overwhelmed them.

In 1891, the character of the plaza changed forever when the white limestone, Renaissance-style city hall replaced the open area in the center of the plaza. Although vendors of many nationalities continued to peddle their wares outside the new city hall, much of the colorful market life moved to Alamo Plaza and to the west, across San Pedro Creek, near the present location of Market Square.

Plaza de las Islas (or Main Plaza as it was called

The elegant Victorian home of the Edward Steves family, 509 King William Street, was completed around 1878 in the German district known at the time as "Sauerkraut Bend." Donated to the Conservation Society in 1953 by the granddaughter of the original owner, the home is open to the public. Thirteen-inch limestone walls, imported mahogany and native walnut woodwork, gracious arches with pierced woodwork details across the porch, and rooms filled with Victorian antiques all make this home a special visit.

The cut-limestone Norton-Polk-Mathis House at 401 King William Street was built in two stages by unknown craftsmen. Russel C. Norton, a hardware merchant, completed the first two stories around 1876, and a few years later new owner Edward Polk, a stockman, added the third-story tower along with a rear wing.

The three-story brick Ellis House at 422 King William Street, built in 1888, is noted for its cylindrical entry porch which extends to the second story and is decorated with richly embellished woodwork.

after independence), immediately to the east of Military Plaza, is the original Villa San Fernando, laid out by the fifty-six Canary Islanders who arrived in 1731 to colonize the new territories for Spain. The majestic San Fernando Cathedral lies between Military and Main plazas. The Islanders laid the cornerstone of the original cathedral in 1738 and finished the building just in time for the visiting Bishop of Guadalajara to confirm the first communion class twenty years later. Paintings and photos reveal a solid Mission-style structure whose dome could be seen miles away by travelers approaching the city from the east.

The new and larger Gothic-style cathedral—the one we see today—was completed in 1872 and was built around the outside of the original so that services would not be interrupted during construction. San Fernando has remained the parish of many San Antonians who trace their ancestry to the Canary Islanders. Each year on March 9, a mass marks another anniversary of the 1731 arrival of these families.

The Bexar County Courthouse, commissioned in 1892 and built of red Texas granite and sandstone, creates a massive presence on the south side of the plaza. The courthouse, with its two towers—one seven stories high with a distinctive beehive spire—reflects the Romanesque style popular at the time.

To the east of Main Plaza and south of River Bend, is the quaint La Villita (Little Village). This historic area, bordered by Alamo, South Presa, Villita, and Nueva streets, features brick- and tile-paved streets, old homes containing shops and studios, restaurants, and a church. You can enter the area from Villita Street just south of the Hilton Hotel or from the River Walk by climbing the step-seats of the Arneson River Theatre. Inside you'll find plazas, meeting halls, historic buildings, and artists' studios and galleries with fine pottery, glass work, jewelry, and woven items on display. The village accommodates celebrations such as Night in Old San Antonio (the Conservation Society's major Fiesta fundraiser), the Starving Artists' Show, Fiesta Noche del Rio, and the lighting of the River Walk Christmas display. The nondenominational Little Church is a favorite for weddings as well as host of one of the city's many charity Thanksgiving dinners.

The La Villita settlement, sometimes mistakenly identified as the first San Antonio settlement, sprang up on mission land south of the Alamo, on a high bluff above the river and close to the best ford—today's Navarro Street. Known originally as the Town of the Alamo, the villa had its own *alcalde,* or mayor, for many years.

After a devastating flood in 1819 that inundated the plaza areas where many of the town's elite citizens lived, the high bluffs of La Villita, which had protected its residents from the flood, attracted new development.

Cos House, a pre-1835 restored stone and stucco house with three rooms opening to the outside, gained its fame from the fact that Martín Perfecto de Cos, was brought here to sign his surrender after the Siege of Béxar in December of 1835. Today the Cos House is often the site of private parties and receptions.

Most of the other Villita edifices were constructed between 1850 and 1900. Small, European-style cottages became interspersed with the Mexican *jacals* and adobes, and probably housed the working people of nineteenth-century San Antonio.

The Villita Ordinance of 1939, under the auspices of Mayor Maury Maverick, established this area as an arts and crafts center; the National Youth Administration and the city provided the funds and labor for restoration.

San Antonio abounds with buildings and homes from the 1850s through the 1900s. Ranging in style and function from the simple dwellings of workers to the elegant Victorian homes of merchants and ranchers, from the ornate city hall and Gothic San Fernando Cathedral to the old German-English school, which survives as a conference center for the Plaza San Antonio Hotel, these are the buildings of the settlers and immigrants who arrived in San Antonio following the Texas Revolution.

Less than a half-mile to the south of La Villita lies the King William area (designated a city historic district in 1967). By the mid-1870s German immigrants represented one-third of the city's population. Ernst Altgelt, a German surveyor and lawyer from Comfort, Texas, moved to San Antonio and planned an elegant community along the river. He laid out three streets parallel to the river south of town and five cross streets. The main avenue was named King William after Kaiser Wilhelm I of Prussia; the parallel streets bore the names of American presidents Washington and Madison.

King William Street was never more than a few blocks long, as C. H. Guenther's immovable Pioneer Flour Mills (now the oldest operating flour-milling

operation in the United States) were located directly across the river. The Guenther House, originally the family home and later a storage area, has undergone renovation and now contains a café and gift shop; the upper floors, filled with beautiful antiques, are open to the public.

The aristocratic families of the city—most, but not all of whom were German ranchers and merchants—built their homes in the King William area in the late 1800s and early 1900s. A stroll through this quiet neighborhood allows you to savor the elegant details and delightful variety of the beautifully restored exteriors—cupolas, verandas, bay windows, wide arches, lacy wood, and iron work. Architecture buffs will recognize styles ranging from Italianate and Monterey Colonial to Gothic and Romanesque Revival.

You can find the headquarters of the San Antonio Conservation Society and its outstanding local history library in an Italianate villa at 107 King William Street, near the corner of South Saint Mary's Street.

Although the private homes in the King William area are not open to the public (except for a tour organized during Fiesta week in April), you may enter the Steves Homestead (at 509 King William Street) for a small fee. Filled with antiques of the late nineteenth century, the interior of the home typifies elegant Victorian decor. It is owned and maintained by the San Antonio Conservation Society.

In addition to the historic King William area, you will find many lovely homes from the early twentieth century in neighborhoods such as Laurel Heights, Monte Vista, Olmos Park, Alamo Heights, and Terrell Hills.

San Antonio has retained and reused a multitude of older buildings, thanks in good part to the efforts of the Conservation Society along with the interest and support of the community at large.

For example, the H.E.B. Company, a South Texas grocery chain, has recently located its headquarters across the river from the King William area on eleven acres of the former U.S. Army arsenal, an active supply depot during the two world wars. Similarly, the San Antonio Museum of Art on Jones

The Kalteyer House at 425 King William Street is one of the few existing residential designs of James Reilly Gordon, who was noted primarily as an architect of county courthouses.

The Wulff House, now the headquarters of the San Antonio Conservation Society and its outstanding local history library, was built in 1878 by Anton Frederick Wulff, who in the 1890s landscaped Alamo Plaza. The Italianate style and asymmetrical design make this an exceptional building.

Avenue resides in a reworked brewery, and the facade of the old Texas Theater has been incorporated into a modern bank building. Even the Johnson Street bridge in the King William area had a former life as the first iron bridge built across the river on Commerce Street (1880).

The French-designed limestone block and rammed earth (*pisé de terre.'*) buildings of the Southwest Craft Center, tucked away on a river bend just north of the city center, served from 1851 until 1965 as the Ursuline Convent and Academy for girls. Late in 1965, the prime riverfront property was rescued from highrise development by the Conservation Society. After some years, the Southwest Craft Center began to occupy and restore the buildings with the help of the Conservation Society and local individuals who appreciated the beauty and history of the property. Today the buildings house classes in weaving, pottery, photography, and papermaking, enrolling as many as five hundred students a semester. Visitors are welcome to view the galleries, shop in the gift shop, and purchase a simple lunch from the Copper Kitchen in the old refectory.

On the north side of Alamo Plaza, the graceful, V-shaped Emily Morgan Hotel, with its Gothic-detailed upper floors, evolved from a Medical Arts Building that at one time housed doctors' offices and a hospital.

The various colleges and universities of San Antonio also feature historic buildings that have been lovingly preserved. San Antonio Community College uses the Koehler House for gallery and meeting space. This ornate Victorian mansion, once the home of Otto Koehler, was built in 1900 and occupies a full

The red-orange brick chapel of the Sisters of Charity of the Incarnate Word, built in 1900, overlooks the campus of Incarnate Word College on Broadway just north of Hildebrand. In the mid-1800s three young women of this French teaching order arrived in San Antonio to assist during a cholera epidemic. Nearly penniless on their arrival, and speaking only French, these stalwart women stayed in San Antonio and by the turn of the century had founded two major San Antonio institutions, Incarnate Word College and Santa Rosa Hospital.

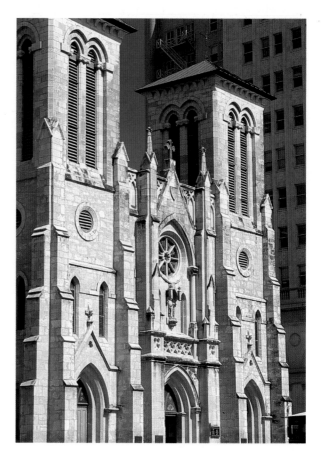

Above left: The Tower Life Building as seen from the river walkway in the King William area. Built in 1929 as the Smith Young Tower, this building was the tallest in San Antonio for almost thirty years. Its lighted green octagonal tower provides a distinctive look to the San Antonio skyline each night. ♦ Above right: Located on the west side of Main Plaza, San Fernando Cathedral was originally the parish church of the Canary Islanders. The cornerstone of the first church on this site was laid in 1738, but it took twenty years to complete the building. The present cathedral, a Gothic Revival design, was erected around the original in 1868 and reopened in 1873. ♦ Left: The Gothic towers of Our Lady of the Lake University add interest to the skyline at 24th and Commerce streets on San Antonio's far west side. Founded by the Sisters of Divine Providence, OLLU provides a variety of programs and innovative scheduling options to the residents of San Antonio and South Texas. Shown here is the Main Building, designed by architect James Wahrenberger, a native Texan of German descent.

The cream-colored, Wahrenberger-designed Administration Building of Saint Mary's University was built far out on the west side in 1894 to house the students of the overcrowded Saint Mary's College (located on the river where La Mansion del Rio Hotel now stands). Three French Brothers of the Society of Mary began their teaching efforts in 1882 in rooms over a livery stable on the west side of Military Plaza. Their determination and efforts blossomed into a 135-acre campus serving over four thousand graduate and undergraduate students. Here thousands of San Antonians have received degrees in the liberal arts, business, and law.

city block.

Though the original Saint Mary's School for boys has been incorporated into La Mansion del Rio Hotel, the later campus located on the far west side boasts an administration building designed by James Wahrenberger and built in 1894. Our Lady of the Lake University contains several magnificent Gothic Revival buildings from the early 1900s also designed by Wahrenberger.

Brackenridge Villa on the Incarnate Word College campus sits on a wooded hill above the San Antonio River headwaters. George Brackenridge, a Scottish real-estate mogul who owned much of what is today Brackenridge Park, Incarnate World College, Fort Sam Houston, and Alamo Heights, purchased this land from Mayor J. R. Sweet and moved into the existing one-story homestead in 1869. As time and money allowed, he built a three-story Queen Anne structure as an addition to the original house.

A few years later, the Sisters of Charity of the Incarnate Word, founders of Santa Rosa Hospital and Incarnate Word College, bought forty acres of the estate, including the villa. Today the restored villa is used by the college for offices and meeting space. Tours of this lovely mansion are available on request.

The red brick bell tower of the Incarnate Word Chapel, built to the east of the villa around 1900, is graced by four angels leaning confidently against each corner to sound their trumpets. Easy to miss as you pass down Broadway, the angels, along with hundreds of other engaging architectural details scattered throughout the city, reward the observant traveler or resident with clues to San Antonio's rich and lively past.

Above: The Italianate Victorian Fairmount Hotel, built in 1906, later attained Guinness Book of Records status as the world's most mobile building after its relocation from the corner of Bowie and Commerce streets to a spot five blocks away near La Villita. For four days in 1985, the city watched as the three-story brick building was jacked onto sixteen dollies and rolled slowly across the San Antonio River to its new location on South Alamo Street. ✦ *Left:* On San Antonio's near west side stands the parish church of Our Lady of Guadalupe, built in 1921 to serve the needs of the thousands of Mexican immigrants who traveled to San Antonio to escape the Mexican Revolution of 1910 and settled along Guadalupe Street. ✦ *Right:* The beautiful Spanish Renaissance–style Southern Pacific Passenger depot, erected in 1903 on the east side of downtown, reflects the elegance and importance of the early days of rail travel. The Beaux Arts interior features a carved-oak-beam, barrel-vault ceiling, art-glass windows, and a skylight. The old station has been spared the demolition ball and now houses the Amtrak Station.

Military

San Antonio is steeped in military tradition and has earned a prominent place in the pages of history. From the Texas War of Independence in the 1800s, the names of Bowie, Crockett, Travis, and Bonham are forever etched in our memories. So should be the name of General Robert E. Lee, who served in San Antonio as the Army Inspector General of Texas just prior to the Civil War. The famous Apache warrior Geronimo also spent time in the city at Post San Antonio, which later became Fort Sam Houston. His stay however, was as a prisoner for forty days in 1886, confined to the watchtower in the Quadrangle while en route to exile at Fort Pickens in Florida. Later in the century, the colorful Teddy Roosevelt formed and trained the First United States Volunteer Calvary, better known as the "Rough Riders," in the San Antonio just prior to action in the Spanish-American War in 1898. And it is important to note that one of America's greatest military figures also called San Antonio home in the 1890s; Douglas MacArthur, whose father Arthur MacArthur was stationed at Fort Sam Houston, attended West Texas Military Institute through 1895.

The advent of the 1900s brought with it the first military airplane flight by an American, Lieutenant Benjamin D. Foulois, from the parade grounds at Fort Sam Houston on March 2, 1910. Foulois flew a Wright Brothers biplane for seven minutes at a maximum altitude of one hundred feet and a top speed of fifty miles per hour. John J. "Black Jack" Pershing used San Antonio as his expedition headquarters just prior to chasing the legendary Pancho Villa in Mexico before World War I. Army Lieutenant Dwight D. Eisenhower married Geneva Ruth "Mamie" Doud while stationed in San Antonio. Lucky Lindy polished his skills here. So did Claire Chennault, later of Flying Tiger fame, and other daredevil aviators such as Frank Hawk, Jimmy Doolittle, and Billy Mitchell. San Antonio was in fact the "mother of the air force." At one time, in 1915, San Antonio was home to the entire United States flying force, which consisted of six reconnaissance planes under the command of then Captain Benjamin D. Foulois and housed at the Fort Sam Houston Airdome.

After being promoted to the rank of major, Foulois was given the opportunity to select a site for a new aviation field in the San Antonio area. On November 21, 1916, he chose a large section of land five miles south of the downtown sector. Construction began in March of 1917, and the first four planes landed there

The clock tower at Fort Sam Houston is located in the Quadrangle at the south entrance to the base. The clock tower is best known as the place Geronimo was held for forty days in 1886 while en route to exile at Florida's Fort Pickens. Today the Quadrangle is surrounded by buildings that serve as headquarters for the Fifth Army; deer, ducks, peacocks, and other animals roam free in the grassy area.

just over a month later on April 5, one day before the United States entered World War I. In June 1917, it was named Kelly Camp in honor of Lieutenant George E. M. Kelly, the first American military aviator to die in a crash of a military plane. Later the installation was called Kelly Field.

Also in 1917, an 873-acre site was chosen and ground was broken for still another flying field on the south side of the city. The United States Army eventually named this facility Brooks Field after Cadet Sidney J. Brooks, a native San Antonian who died in a flight-training crash at Kelly Field on November 13, 1917. The first airplanes flown at Brooks were the famous Curtiss JN-4s, commonly known as "Jennies" and used extensively in World War I. Sixteen hangars were constructed to house the flying fleet, with one remaining today. It's Hangar Nine, now used for the Edward H. White II Memorial Museum of space travel and flight medicine.

One of the most remarkable periods in the history of Brooks Field came between 1919 and 1922. Pilot training gave way to a balloon and airship school. A massive 91,000-square-foot balloon hangar was constructed for huge hydrogen-filled dirigibles. Both pilots and ground crew were trained at Brooks until several mishaps in operating the balloons caused the army to abandon the effort. After this, Brooks once again became a flying school for the U.S. Army Air Corps and headquarters for the School of Aviation Medicine.

Other highlights in the early histories of Kelly and Brooks fields included the 1927 filming at Kelly of *Wings,* the only silent movie to ever receive an Oscar award for best picture, and the first successful paratrooper drop in September of 1929 at Brooks.

Fort Sam Houston, Kelly Field, and Brooks Field were followed in San Antonio's military history by Randolph Field, dedicated on June 20, 1930. Randolph was originally known as the "West Point of the air," because of its designation as the primary flying training wing for the United States Army Air Corp and later for the United States Air Force. Randolph Field was named after Captain William M. Randolph, a native of Austin who earned recognition as

a remarkable aviator in his eleven-year flying career. Of special interest at Randolph is the "Taj Mahal," a 148-foot building-tower that originally served as administration headquarters for the base upon its opening in October 1931. The "Taj Mahal" nickname comes from its slight resemblance to the shrine in India and from the tower's blue and gold mosaic dome.

The last of San Antonio's five military installations, Lackland Army Air Base, came on line in 1941. U.S. involvement in World War II gave Lackland its continuing role, that of training recruits. Throughout World War II, the Korean Conflict, and the Vietnam War, Lackland was heavily depended on to train millions of young men and women. Maybe this is why Lackland, later to be renamed Lackland Air Force Base, is still known today as the "gateway to the air force."

These five major military installations continue operations in San Antonio today. Fort Sam Houston is headquarters for the Fifth U.S. Army which covers a fourteen-state territory. Brooke General Hospital, one of the largest military medical facilities in the world, is located here and specializes in the treatment of burns. The Academy of Health Sciences coordinates all army medical training in the United States from its base of operations at Fort Sam Houston. All air fields and army air bases are now air force bases, but the names remain the same. Kelly is the largest maintenance installation in the air force, employing thousands of military and civil service personnel. It is also headquarters for the U.S. Air Force Security Service. Brooks features the School of Aerospace Medicine, which provides valuable research and assistance to the national space program. Randolph continues as home to Air Training Command. Lackland remains the largest processing and training center for recruits and officer candidates in the air force. Its Wilford Hall Hospital is the largest of all air force medical facilities.

San Antonio is proud of its military heritage. The Alamo City is the largest military complex in the United States outside the Washington, D.C., area.

Randolph Air Force Base's administrative offices are housed in the "Taj Mahal," named for its similarities to the shrine in India. Randolph Air Force Base is known as "the West Point of the air" because of its importance as a pilot-training center.

Open House at Kelly Air Force Base is a special occasion for thousands of San Antonians and South Texans. Once a year, visitors are invited to tour the facility and are treated to a fabulous air show, usually featuring the Thunderbirds, the Air Force's precision flying team. This event gives people the opportunity to get an up-close look at the most current airplanes in the fleet, including this C-5 cargo plane.

Lackland Air Force Base is known as "the Gateway to the Air Force" because it is the largest recruit-training facility in the United States. Shown here is a portion of a parade ground on the base and a vintage World War II airplane. The entire exhibit is comprised of approximately twenty World War II planes.

The Vietnam Memorial depicts a soldier helping a fallen comrade at the battle of Hill 881 South. Created by sculptor Austin Deuel, the Vietnam Memorial stands as a remembrance of all who lost their lives in the Vietnam Conflict. It was financed by the private contributions of approximately 130,000 people.

Parks &
Museums

San Antonio offers a healthy variety of museums with permanent exhibits of traditional and contemporary art, regional history, popular culture, and natural sciences. Parks run the gamut from the picnic table, merry-go-round variety to a botanical center devoted to the cultivation and study of exotic as well as indigenous plants. The zoo exhibits animals from all around the world. Increasingly, these institutions are engaging in a mix of educational and outreach activities guaranteed to appeal to the interests of the community at large. Whether you're visiting San Antonio for a few days or have lived here a lifetime, you'll find a multitude of places to discover and explore.

Each of San Antonio's museums has a different flavor and focus, as well as its own history. The San Antonio Museum of Art (SAMA) occupies the former turn-of-the-century Lone Star Brewery on Jones Avenue. Built in 1903 by Adolphus Busch of Saint Louis, the brewery churned out barrels of beer until prohibition in the 1920s. At that point, it was converted into a cotton mill, and then transformed into the Lone Star Ice and Food Store. During the next fifty years, the brewery complex served as warehouse space. But in the early 1970s, the museum board rescued it, purchasing five of the buildings and beginning renovation.

For the most part, the exterior remains true to its original style. However, architects reworked the interior into gallery space that is at once handsome and functional. The museum earned a design award from *Progressive Architecture* magazine and was recognized by *Time* as one of the five best designs of 1981. A glassed-in catwalk connects two four-story towers, overlooking the downtown San Antonio skyline on one side and the northern suburbs on the other. As they rise, glass elevators in the towers entice visitors with views of the exhibits on each floor. Although the sixteen galleries feature many changing exhibits, some of the outstanding permanent collections include Mexican folk art, Chinese ceramics, Pre-Columbian and Spanish Colonial art, as well as the START Gallery—a hands-on art experience for young people. The new Ewing Halsell Wing for Ancient Art opened in 1990 and contains the most comprehensive collection of antiquities shown in the Southwest, illustrating Egyptian, Greek, and Roman art. During the summer of 1991, SAMA was one of three U.S. museums chosen to display "Mexico: Splendors of Thirty Centuries," the largest and most important

Pathways wind around the base of an old quarry, guiding walkers among the colorful plantings of the Japanese Tea Gardens. Located in an abandoned quarry area that once contained the first cement plant west of the Mississippi, the gardens, in the northwest quadrant of Brackenridge, can be reached by park roadway or by the aerial skyride.

Red and orange canna lilies outline the pool and fountain facing the main entrance of the Marion Koogler McNay Museum. Lovers of art, architecture, and beautiful landscaping will find this museum one of the loveliest spots in San Antonio. In addition, serious students of art and theater will be drawn to the extensive library facility. Additions to the original three-story Spanish Colonial Revival–style house, built in 1927, have allowed the museum to expand and display its excellent collection, making it one of the finest small museums in the United States.

exhibition of Mexican art ever assembled.

On the east side of Brackenridge Park, you'll find the Witte Museum, a family museum featuring exhibits of Texas natural science, history, and anthropology. Children especially enjoy the popular dinosaur exhibit; history buffs will be interested in the Witte's three restored historic homes, relocated from other parts of the city. The Twohig and Navarro houses are furnished with handcrafted furniture and accessories created by regional craftspeople — churns, bowls, quilts, handwoven fabrics, embroideries, and wrought iron fireplace tools.

The John Twohig House, the first two-story house in San Antonio, was built by an industrious, though eccentric, Irish merchant and prominent citizen who ran a store on Main Plaza. Among Twohig's endeavors was the establishment of the first breadline in America. Each morning he and his family issued loaves of bread to the women of poor San Antonio families. Twohig also went to unusual lengths to prevent the stock of gunpowder in his store from falling into the hands of Mexican invaders in 1842 — he detonated the entire shop!

The Twohigs entertained many notable personalities of the day in their home on the river. Included were Robert E. Lee, Sam Houston, and Ulysses S. Grant. The Witte has painstakingly reassembled the original fireplace, mantles, door, and walls on the museum grounds.

The Francisco Ruiz House, originally situated on the south side of Military Plaza, was built before 1765 and functioned as a school in the early 1800s. During the Battle of the Alamo, Colonel Ruiz's son acted as mayor of the city and was responsible for disposing of the slain Mexicans and Texans.

In addition to its many exhibits, the Witte Museum enriches the community's intellectual life by providing a diverse menu of lectures, trips, and hands-on activities for adults as well as children.

The McNay Art Museum sits atop a hill in Northeast San Antonio surrounded by twenty-five rolling acres of landscaped gardens, sculptures, and fountains. Marion Koogler McNay bequeathed the Spanish Colonial Revival–style building, constructed in 1929, along with her extensive art collection, which focused on first-generation post-impressionists and American watercolorists, to the museum association. Generous gifts from the community have enabled the museum to expand its collection and its space. New

Above: A replica of an 1863 Central Pacific Huntington Steam Engine pulls the one-fifth-scale model Brackenridge passenger train across a specially constructed bridge over the San Antonio River. Tracks cover three miles of wooded and open area, crossing the river twice and allowing stops at four stations around the park. ◆ *Left: A scarlet ibis suns itself against the rock walls of the old stone quarry that houses much of the San Antonio Zoo. Maintained by the San Antonio Zoological Society, the zoo continues to expand its holdings and rework exhibits so that animals may dwell in the most natural of habitats.*

galleries house permanent and changing exhibits. The Tobin Wing, opened in 1984, houses an eight-thousand-volume library on theater arts, as well as an extensive fine arts research library on the lower level.

Since 1985, the Blue Star Art Complex, a sprawling warehouse area built in the 1920s for cold storage and located on the river not far from the King William area, has provided studio as well as exhibit space for contemporary artists.

If your enthusiasms lean toward museums of the outdoor variety, take a picnic to one of San Antonio's parks, where you can view the impressive diversity of South Texas flora, examine exotic cacti and the trees of the tropical rain forest, or walk among an ever-expanding collection of the world's animal species.

San Pedro Park remains of historic, rather than current, interest, as the springs dried up in 1950. However, it is the second oldest municipal park in the United States—the Boston Commons being the oldest—and once contained the headwaters of San Pedro Creek. The land was set aside for community use by the King of Spain in 1734. During the late nineteenth century, this park was a popular picnic spot, although visitors risked being attacked by Comanches as late as 1860. Today, the park contains the McFarland Tennis Center and the San Pedro Park Playhouse, whose facade is a replica of the old Market House, razed in 1925.

Brackenridge Park is probably the city's most traditional park. George Brackenridge, president of the Water Works Company, deeded a major part of the park to the city in 1899. The park consists of a number of attractions spread over 370 acres. Woods and winding trails for horseback riding cover the southern half of the park, while the San Antonio River meanders through the northern half, passing picnic pavilions which can be reserved for special occasions. Paddleboats, a carousel with antique horses, ball fields, rental horses, and a driving range make Brackenridge a favorite family gathering place on weekends and special holidays such as Easter and July Fourth. The miniature Brackenridge Park Railroad winds through the park, stopping at several stations where visitors can board or get off to explore. An aerial skyride offers a sweeping view of the park, the downtown skyline, nearby Trinity University, and the San Antonio River.

The San Antonio Zoo, built into quarries from which the early Spaniards hauled stone for their houses, holds the third largest collection of animals in the United States. The exhibit areas, built against the backdrop of the limestone cliffs of the abandoned quarries, simulate natural habitats wherever possible. Towering oaks, pecan, and cypress trees shade strollers in the heat of summer; the water running through the zoo is part of an irrigation ditch left over from the city's mission days.

The Japanese Tea Gardens, located in the northwest corner of Brackenridge Park, occupy another rock quarry, one that produced limestone for the state capitol in Austin. A cool spot in spring and summer, the gardens overflow with hundreds of varieties of plants on either side of the path wandering past ponds and fountains. The kiln and houses for quarry workers can still be seen today. An outdoor theater to the west of the garden offers concerts, the summer Shakespeare festival, and Fiesta events such as a Taste of New Orleans.

HemisFair Park is the downtown site of the magical 1968 World's Fair, an event that brought the world to San Antonio's doorstep for a little while. During the fair's six months of operation, six million visitors flooded the city to see over ninety acres of exhibits housed in buildings constructed by citizens from twenty-five nations. HemisFair commemorated San Antonio's 250th year; to mark the twentieth anniversary of HemisFair in 1988, the city built a water park near the Tower of the Americas. Here, fountains, water cascades, and pools provide a refreshing stop on a warm San Antonio day. One of the most breathtaking views of the city can be found at the top of the tallest structure in the city, the 750-foot Tower of the Americas; the restaurant and observation decks rotate once each hour.

Another permanent fixture of HemisFair Park, the Institute of Texan Cultures, offers a rich insight into the diverse peoples of the state. Owned by the University of Texas, the museum's mission is to preserve and tell the stories of settlers from all over the world who made Texas their home. In addition to sponsoring the annual Texas Folklife Festival each August, the museum maintains a library, traveling exhibits and programs for schools, and an extensive photographic collection.

Part of a major urban renewal project, the clearing of the ninety acres for HemisFair destroyed many

Left: Two black-bellied ducks survey the pond at the north end of the thirty-three acres that comprise the San Antonio Botanical Center. In addition to the formal gardens, each of three Texas vegetative regions—the piney woods of East Texas, the plains of South Texas, and the Central Texas Hill Country—are represented by indigenous varieties of trees, soils, grasses, and plants. ◆ Above: Snapdragons and salvia provide a blaze of color amid lush greenery in the courtyard of the Lucile Halsell Conservatory at the San Antonio Botanical Center. Its one-half acre under glass makes it the largest conservatory in the Southwest. ◆ Right: The award-winning Lucile Halsell Conservatory has been specifically designed to shelter ferns, tropicals, palms, arctic plants, and other exotics from the debilitating heat and dryness of the South Texas climate. Tentlike glass pavilions extend sixteen feet underground where paths take visitors to the various exhibit rooms around the beautifully landscaped courtyard and pool.

historic buildings. Others were saved and used as fair buildings. Exhibit halls built for the fair are now a familiar part of downtown San Antonio. Today, the HemisFair area contains the Convention Center with its arena and concert hall, the National Autonomous University of Mexico, the Instituto Cultural Mexicano, as well as an extension of Texas A&M Engineering School, and the renovated Beethoven Hall. The circular United States Pavilion became the John H. Wood, Jr. United States Courthouse. In 1989 volunteers from all over the city generously provided design, materials, and construction for an innovative playground located in the southwest corner of the HemisFair area.

The relatively new San Antonio Botanical Gardens on the north side of the city off North New Braunfels Avenue offers thirty-three acres of exemplary Texas landscapes, as well as Japanese Gardens (not to be confused with the Tea Gardens in Brackenridge Park), historic buildings, and a conservatory. Built on land that once belonged to the Brackenridge waterworks and reservoir of the 1890s, the grounds are in a state of continuing development. An old-fashioned garden demonstrates the annuals and perennials used by Texas pioneers, while the Sacred Gardens reach back even further, displaying oleander, pomegranate, myrtle, fig, and other plants cultivated during Biblical times.

Fifteen acres of land are devoted to native Texas plants representing three distinctly different vegetational regions of the state: the Hill Country, the East Texas Pineywoods, and the South Texas Plains. A one-acre xeriscape exhibit shows a variety of native and imported plants combined with irrigation techniques that use minimal amounts of water. The children's garden program enables children to grow and harvest vegetables from their own organic plots. The bermed greenhouses of the Lucille Halsell Conservatory complex grow tropical and desert plants of the New World; its one-half acre under glass makes it the largest conservatory in the Southwest. Other gardens include the Garden for the Blind, with highly textured plants identified by braille plaques, and the Japanese garden given by San Antonio's sister city—Kumamoto, Japan—as a gesture of friendship. The stone walks, ponds, waterfalls, and bamboo fences surround a copper-roofed tea house where guests may sit and relax. Finally, the Sullivan Carriage House, moved one stone at a time from its original location at Broadway and Fourth Street, reflects turn-of-the-century architecture. When restored, its interior will house a gift shop, tea room, and lecture hall.

Early morning sunlight, suggesting the heat of the day to come, falls on the thick walls of a limestone Hill Country house—one of three authentic early Texas dwellings featured at the San Antonio Botanical Center. A wooden East Texas house with wrap-around porch sits at the north end of the pond, while the South Texas adobe with prickly pear cactus growing on the sod roof is exhibited in the brush country area.

Entertainment
& Festivals

The age of formal entertainment and performing arts really began in San Antonio in 1886 with the completion of the Grand Opera House on Alamo Plaza. This outstanding edifice was heralded as one of the finest performing arts venues in the nation at the time. Edwin Thomas Booth, brother of the infamous assassin of Lincoln John Wilkes Booth, performed there. So did Sarah Bernhardt. Sadly, its existence was short-lived.

In April 1891, a lasting tradition was born in San Antonio: Fiesta. Women from the San Antonio Club decided to organize a parade to honor the heroes of the Alamo and San Jacinto, the battle in which Texas won its independence from Mexico in 1836. The parade was first scheduled for April 21, San Jacinto Day, but was changed to April 20 when the women learned President Benjamin Harrison would visit the Alamo City on that day. The theme of the event was the "Battle of Flowers," inspired by the flower carnivals of France and Mexico and the parades of Germany. But it rained on April 20, forcing postponement of the grand affair. Even though the president had already left town, the parade, held four days later, was deemed an overwhelming success. Amid the pomp and dignity of bands, horsemen, floats, and carriages ensued the throwing of flowers between parade participants. People were pelted, pelted back, and loved it. Over one hundred years later, the Battle of Flowers Parade is still the focal point of the ten-day celebration in April that we now call Fiesta San Antonio. Hundreds of thousands of people line the streets to catch a glimpse of beautiful flower-covered floats, marching bands, and kings, queens, and duchesses—royalty for the moment. Through the years, two more parades have been added to Fiesta: the Texas Cavaliers' River Parade and the Fiesta Flambeau Parade, both evening events.

Fiesta is food, fun, and celebration. It is a coming together of San Antonians and visitors alike. Many meet at NIOSA, "A Night in Old San Antonio," held annually at La Villita. This four-night extravaganza features a never-ending array of food booths, music, dancing, games, and merriment. La Villita means "Little Town," and that it is. During peak hours, the volume of revelers overwhelms the size of the area. A sea of people celebrates. It's part of the charm of NIOSA.

Hundreds of other events are held during the ten-day party at locations throughout the city. From 1891

The list of famous personalities who have performed at the Majestic Theater on Houston Street since 1926 is virtually endless. Recently, this magnificent hall was restored to its original elegance through the efforts of the Las Casas Foundation. Today, it is home to the San Antonio Symphony and the Majestic Broadway Series, and is a favorite venue for individual performances.

This Mexican Rodeo participant's sombrero enhances her classic Hispanic beauty.

A sea of San Antonians and Fiesta visitors crowds its way into La Villita for each of the four nights of NIOSA, Night in Old San Antonio. NIOSA is a feast of food, fun, dancing, music, and games.

Fiesta San Antonio, a ten-day, city-wide celebration held in April, features three parades. Fiesta Flambeau, a night parade, lights up the downtown streets with excitement and beauty; the Texas Cavaliers' River Parade, also held at night, features decorated barges; and the oldest and biggest of them all, the Battle of Flowers Parade, is a daytime event that attracts over 300,000 spectators annually.

The Arneson River Theater plays host to Fiesta Noche del Rio (Night Party on the River) every Tuesday night during the summer months. The Arneson stage, on the north side of the San Antonio River, is filled with exceptional Hispanic singing and dancing, while spectators watch from grass-covered terraced steps on the south side of the waterway. Connecting them is Rosita's Bridge, a walkway named after Rosita Fernandez, a legendary Fiesta Noche del Rio performer. Barges float between the performers and the crowd.

to the present, Fiesta San Antonio has become one of the largest city celebrations in America, rivaled only by New Orleans's Mardi Gras.

The 1890s also brought San Antonio one of the most magnificent concert halls for musical and vocal performances in the Southwest. Beethoven Hall, located on South Alamo Street, was conceived, created, and completed in 1895 by the Beethoven Maennerchor, a German singing society. Unlike the Grand Opera House, which met with demolition, Beethoven Hall remains in use today.

The next great influence on entertainment in San Antonio came in the 1920s with the opening of two movie-vaudeville palaces. The Majestic Theater on Houston Street, a Moorish design by John Eberson, and the Aztec Theater on Saint Mary's Street at Commerce, opened in 1929. Both were large-capacity houses that featured silent movies and "talkies" as well as live stage performances. Today, the Majestic has been magnificently restored to its original grandeur by Las Casas Foundation and is currently the home of the San Antonio Symphony, touring Broadway plays, and other performing arts events. The Aztec Theater is dark and awaits renovation and a new life.

The Majestic and Aztec weren't the only theaters of the era, just the most incredible ones. As a matter of fact, in the 1920s theaters lined the downtown streets in great numbers. Their names seem symbolic of this golden age of entertainment: the Palace, the Prince, the Bijou, the Strand, the State, the Texas, the Rialto, the Rivoli, and the Royal, to list a few. Regrettably, they are gone. The only reminder of their existence is the Texas Theater front which stands as a part of a large bank building on Houston Street.

Another of the Alamo City's most loved events had its beginning in March 1928. It was called the International Exposition and Livestock Show. This was the forerunner to our current San Antonio Stock Show & Rodeo, which occupies ten days of our lives every February. The Joe & Harry Freeman Coliseum, after its completion in 1949, became the permanent venue for this country and western showcase. All the real cowboys and cowgirls, and the drugstore kind too, show up to see top-notch entertainers, bucking broncos, snorting bulls, very fast clowns, the midway, and more. Probably more boots, hats, and western duds are sold to tinhorns during the thirty days leading up to the rodeo than during all the other months combined. Ride 'em cowboy!

The San Antonio Symphony Society was next in the city's future. Organized in September 1939, the symphony has provided San Antonio with some of its greatest classical and popular music moments. Its service to the patrons of the city has been extremely consistent through the years. At present, the symphony calls the Majestic Theater home. The theater itself is a masterpiece of architectural and acoustical achievement. Add the beautiful music performed by the symphony, and you have magic.

And speaking of magic, when the sun rose over San Antonio on April 6, 1968, a wonderful world of excitement came to life. HemisFair '68, San Antonio's World's Fair, ushered in a new era for the city. Ninety-two acres of downtown property had been transformed into the most colorful and festive exposition imaginable. San Antonio invited the peoples of the world to our party. And they came, by the millions. For HemisFair, the city built the much-needed HemisFair Arena and the Lila Cockrell Theater for the Performing Arts complex. Thousands of live performances have been held there since opening, including the legendary singer Frank Sinatra and operatic tenor Luciano Pavarotti, the Bolshoi and the Joffrey ballets, and dance luminaries Mikhail Baryshnikov and Rudolf Nureyev.

Many performances have been sponsored by the San Antonio Performing Arts Association (SAPAA), a group formed in 1978. SAPAA has been responsible for bringing the world's talent to San Antonio's stages. So has its counterpart, the San Antonio Festival. Since the early 1980s, the Festival has filled the month of June with wonderful performances that span the cultural arts.

Fiesta, the rodeo, the symphony, SAPAA, and the Festival are joined by many other arts and entertainment groups in the city, as well as other festivals, in amusing, regaling, and enriching the lives of San Antonio patrons. The Majestic Broadway Series is always a season of highlights. Sea World features big-name entertainment, in addition to the biggest name, Shamu the killer whale. Fiesta Texas is music, music, music. San Antonians and visitors also enjoy the Texas Folklife Festival at the Institute of Texan Cultures. Held annually in August, it's a celebration featuring the arts, crafts, music, dancing, and lifestyles of the twenty-six nationalities who settled Texas. The

The women of "The Light Brigade" are easy to spot. Their yellow wide-brimmed straw hats and yellow dresses identify them as members of the exclusive Battle of Flowers Association, the organization that started Fiesta San Antonio in 1891.

Carver Cultural Center presents an extensive array of performances annually, as does the Guadalupe Cultural Arts Center. Local theater is alive and well at several venues in the Alamo City.

San Antonio is a not only a city of fiestas; it's also a city of feasts! Although San Antonio is best known for its Mexican food, many other culinary influences exist. Diners throughout the city also enjoy the tasteful traditions of such peoples as the Germans, French, Italians, Polish, Greeks, Lebanese, and Asians. The palates of millions of annual visitors and locals alike savor the San Antonio culinary experience.

Nevertheless, Mexican food is royalty in San Antonio. The charm of the River Walk, the Alamo, and the missions lure people to the city, but it's the native food and fun that make them want to stay. While listening to the musical strains of mariachis, many experience a taco, tamale, or tostada for the first time. In fact, Mexican food as we know it in San Antonio may be America's best-kept culinary secret. We call it "Tex-Mex," a cuisine that has evolved through the years with both Texan and Mexican characteristics. You won't find it in any state in the union except Texas. As a matter of fact, Tex-Mex, in its purest form, is served only in South Texas, with San Antonio harboring its finest kitchens.

Mexican food restaurants can be found in every area of the city, from the River Walk and El Mercado to hotels and downtown streets to cozy corners and neighborhoods to malls and the expanses of suburbia. If you are a visitor, sample and savor at one, two, or a few. If you are a native San Antonian or South Texan, continue your never-ending search for the absolute best.

Above: Fiesta Texas calls itself "the biggest, brightest celebration under the great Lone Star." A joint venture between San Antonio–based USAA (an insurance company that serves military and retired military personnel worldwide) and Opryland USA of Nashville, Fiesta Texas is a combination of thrilling amusement park rides and energetic live musical entertainment. The park is divided into five areas: Los Festivales, Ol' Waterin' Hole, Crackaxle Canyon, Rockville, and Spassburg. ◆ Left: Fiesta Texas is the home of The Rattler, the world's tallest wooden rollercoaster.

Left: First you hear the sizzle; then you see the steam. Ampy Calvillo serves fajitas at Cappy's, an Alamo City restaurant. San Antonio is the headquarters for Tex-Mex, a cuisine that has evolved through generations of Hispanic cooking, featuring the blending of flavors from Texas and Mexico. ◆ Above: Originally built by publisher Harcourt Brace Jovanovich, Sea World of Texas is now owned by the Anheuser-Busch Company. It is the largest Sea World in the United States; others are located in San Diego, Orlando, and Cleveland. Visitors to the park are treated to shows by dolphins, killer whales, sea lions, walruses, and other marine species, and exhibits include penguins and sharks. ◆ Right: Confetti flies as a cascarone is cracked on the head. This hand-painted egg shell filled with bits of colorful paper is a tradition at Easter and during Fiesta. To make a cascarone, peck a hole in the end of an egg, drain, dry, then stuff with confetti.

Reflections

We have painted a verbal and visual picture, a portrait, of San Antonio and its place in history. It is the Alamo City, "cradle of Texas liberty," the home of the River Walk, the mother of the air force, and "one of America's four unique cities," along with New Orleans, San Francisco, and Boston. The people who live here should be proud of their city's heritage. We believe they are. The people who visit here should be captivated by San Antonio's charm. We believe they are.

"Solamente en San Antonio." From Fiesta San Antonio and the Texas Folklife Festival to the San Antonio Stock Show & Rodeo and the Texas Conjunto Festival to Fiesta Noche del Rio and the San Antonio Festival of Performing Arts to any day of the year, it's nonstop entertainment, food, and fun. San Antonio has character. It's a great place to visit, but a better place to live.

Mexican Rodeo is a favorite Sunday afternoon tradition enjoyed by many San Antonians and visitors. Cowboys, known as charros, perform in a series of riding and roping events unlike those of Old West rodeoing. It's a very colorful and spirited occasion.

Selected Readings

Carson, C. and W. McDonald. *Guide to San Antonio Architecture.* San Antonio Chapter of AIA, 1986.

Davis, J. L. *San Antonio: a Historical Portrait.* Austin: Encino Press, 1978.

Foster, N. *Texas Monthly Guide to San Antonio.* Houston: Gulf Publishing, 1989

Guerra, M. A. *The Alamo.* San Antonio: Alamo Press, 1983.

_____. *History of San Antonio's Market Square.* San Antonio: Alamo Press, 1988.

_____. *The Missions of San Antonio.* San Antonio: Alamo Press, 1982.

_____. *The San Antonio River.* San Antonio: Alamo Press, 1987.

Poyo, G., and G. Hinojosa, eds. *Tejano Origins in Eighteenth Century San Antonio.* Austin: University of Texas Press, 1991.

Ramsdell, C. *San Antonio: A Historical and Pictorial Guide.* 2d ed. Austin: University of Texas Press, 1985.

Zunker, V. G. *A Dream Come True: Robert Hugman and San Antonio's River Walk.* (Out of print.)